Emilie PLASSIN

Emerging Congress Destinations

Charles Seale-Hayne Library
University of Plymouth
(01752) 588 588
LibraryandITenquiries@plymouth.ac.uk

Emilie PLASSIN

Emerging Congress Destinations

Key factors of success and future trends, on example of the cities of Lille and Linz

VDM Verlag Dr. Müller

Impressum/Imprint (nur für Deutschland/ only for Germany)
Bibliografische Information der Deutschen Nationalbibliothek: Die Deutsche Nationalbibliothek verzeichnet diese Publikation in der Deutschen Nationalbibliografie; detaillierte bibliografische Daten sind im Internet über http://dnb.d-nb.de abrufbar.
Alle in diesem Buch genannten Marken und Produktnamen unterliegen warenzeichen-, marken- oder patentrechtlichem Schutz bzw. sind Warenzeichen oder eingetragene Warenzeichen der jeweiligen Inhaber. Die Wiedergabe von Marken, Produktnamen, Gebrauchsnamen, Handelsnamen, Warenbezeichnungen u.s.w. in diesem Werk berechtigt auch ohne besondere Kennzeichnung nicht zu der Annahme, dass solche Namen im Sinne der Warenzeichen- und Markenschutzgesetzgebung als frei zu betrachten wären und daher von jedermann benutzt werden dürften.

Coverbild: www.purestockx.com

Verlag: VDM Verlag Dr. Müller Aktiengesellschaft & Co. KG
Dudweiler Landstr. 99, 66123 Saarbrücken, Deutschland
Telefon +49 681 9100-698, Telefax +49 681 9100-988, Email: info@vdm-verlag.de

Herstellung in Deutschland:
Schaltungsdienst Lange o.H.G., Berlin
Books on Demand GmbH, Norderstedt
Reha GmbH, Saarbrücken
Amazon Distribution GmbH, Leipzig
ISBN: 978-3-639-10977-1

Imprint (only for USA, GB)
Bibliographic information published by the Deutsche Nationalbibliothek: The Deutsche Nationalbibliothek lists this publication in the Deutsche Nationalbibliografie; detailed bibliographic data are available in the Internet at http://dnb.d-nb.de.
Any brand names and product names mentioned in this book are subject to trademark, brand or patent protection and are trademarks or registered trademarks of their respective holders. The use of brand names, product names, common names, trade names, product descriptions etc. even without a particular marking in this works is in no way to be construed to mean that such names may be regarded as unrestricted in respect of trademark and brand protection legislation and could thus be used by anyone.

Cover image: www.purestockx.com

Publisher:
VDM Verlag Dr. Müller Aktiengesellschaft & Co. KG
Dudweiler Landstr. 99, 66123 Saarbrücken, Germany
Phone +49 681 9100-698, Fax +49 681 9100-988, Email: info@vdm-verlag.de

Copyright © 2008 by the author and VDM Verlag Dr. Müller Aktiengesellschaft & Co. KG and licensors
All rights reserved. Saarbrücken 2008

Printed in the U.S.A.
Printed in the U.K. by (see last page)
ISBN: 978-3-639-10977-1

Emerging congress destinations

Key factors of success and future trends, on example of the cities of Lille and Linz

Diploma Thesis

submitted at the

IMC University of Applied Sciences Krems

Degree-Programme/Diplomstudiengang

„Tourism & Leisure Management"

by

Emilie PLASSIN

for the award of the academic degree

MAGISTER (FH) / MAGISTRA (FH)

für wirtschaftswissenschaftliche Berufe

Thesis Coach: Mixner, Hans

Submitted on: 19.05.2008

"I declare in lieu of an oath that I have written this diploma thesis myself and that I have not used any sources or resources other than stated for its preparation. I further declare that I have clearly indicated all direct and indirect quotations. This diploma thesis has not been submitted elsewhere for examination purposes."

Date: 19/05/2008

ABSTRAKT

Die Branche des Geschäftstourismus und ganz speziell die der Kongressindustrie nehmen immer mehr an Bedeutung zu.

Das Ziel dieser Untersuchung ist es, die wichtigsten Erfolgsfaktoren und Zukunftstrends für aufstrebende Kongressdestinationen an Hand der beiden Beispielstädte Linz und Lille, zu verdeutlichen.

Diese Diplomarbeit versucht, einen bedeutenden Aspekt der Kongressindustrie, nämlich den der Schlüsselfaktoren für eine neu entstehende Destination, ihre Konkurrenzfähigkeit und Attraktivität durch gründliche Nachforschung, verbunden mit Wissensaustausch mit der betroffenen Sparte, zu erklären.

Das Endergebnis der Forschung soll das Erlangen von Information zu Infrastruktur, Organisation von Institutionen, Angeboten und Kunden/Organisatoren Motivation in der Kongressbranche sein.

Persönliche Meinungen und Vorstellungen zu Zukunftsperspektiven für Lille und Linz werden gesammelt.

Die Analyse der beiden Orte basiert nicht nur auf Primär- sondern auch Sekundärdaten. Die Autorin wird sowohl quantitative als auch qualitative Daten verwenden, indem sie diese ermittelt und gegenüberstellt, durch die Untersuchung von Marketing, Logistik, Attraktivität und Konkurrenzfähigkeit. Um dieses Ergebnis zu erreichen, hat die Autorin Interviews geführt und Angaben von Fachkreisen gesammelt.

Das persönliche Interesse der Autorin an der Kongressbranche ist stark angestiegen infolge eines Praktikums bei Maison de la France, wo sie erfahren hat, wie ein Land durch Marketing und Pressearbeit abgesetzt wird.

Im Zuge der vergangenen Semester an der Fachhochschule IMC Krems hatte sie die Möglichkeit, Vertiefungen in Richtung Geschäftstourismus zu besuchen und den Wunsch zu entwickeln, mehr Wissen und Fähigkeiten in diesem Feld zu erlangen.

ABSTRACT

The business industry and particularly the congress industry are gaining more and more importance in the tourism industry.

The purpose of this investigation is to clarify the key factors of success and the future trends for an emerging congress destination, using the example of the two cities of Linz and Lille.

This diploma thesis will try to explain an aspect of the congress industry, namely which are the keys factors of an emerging destination, its competitiveness and attractiveness through intensive research, coupled with an exchange of information with industry.

The objective of the research is to obtain information on infrastructure, institutions-organizations, offers and client/organizer motivation in the congress branch.

Personal opinions and ideas of future perspectives of Lille and Linz will be collected.

The analysis of the destinations is based on both primary and secondary data. The author will use both quantitative and qualitative data by determining and confronting these different ones, by analyzing the marketing, the logistic part as well as the attractiveness and competitiveness. To reach its objective the author has conducted some interviews and collected data from professionals of the trade.

The author's interest in the congress branch increased as the result of an internship at Maison de la France where she learnt about the way how to promote a country through marketing and press.

During the past semesters at the IMC Krems, University of Applied Sciences she had the opportunity to attend business tourism modules and developed a will to acquire more skills and knowledge in this domain.

TABLE OF CONTENTS

LIST OF FIGURES

LIST OF TABLES

LIST OF ABBREVIATIONS

ACI   Airports Council International

ACBN   Austrian Business and Convention Network

AGM   Annual General Meetings

AIPC   Association internationale des palais des congrès

ANTO   Austrian National Tourist Office

APIM   Agence pour la promotion Internationale de Lille Metropole

ASAE   American Society of Association Executives

CCI   Chamber of Commerce and Industry

CRM   Customer Relationship Management

DMAI   Destination Marketing Association International

DMC   Destination Management Company

DMO   Destination Marketing Organizations

DOME   Data on Meetings and Events

DRIS   Digitales Oberösterreichisches Raum Information System

ECM   European Cities Marketing

FMEL   Federal Ministry of Economics and Labor

GIX   Global Internet Exchange

IAPCO   international association of professional congress organizer

ICCA   International Congress and Convention Association

INSEE   National Institute for Statistics and Economic Studies

JKU   Johannes Kepler Universität

KEP   Kulturentwicklungsplan

MICE   Meeting, Incentive, Conference, Event

MPI   Meeting professional international

NIIP   National Institute of Industrial Property

NTIC   New technologies and information communication

ODIT   Tourism engineering observatory and organization

ÖGAF   Österreichische Gesellschaft für angewandte Fremdenverkehrswirtschaft

ÖW   Österreich Werbung

PCMA   professional convention management association

PCO   Professional Conference Organizer

SAEM Société anonyme d'économie mixte

SEM   Société d'économie mixte – Mixed economy company

TGV   Train Grande Vitesse

UIA   Union of International Associations

UCLM Urban Community of Lille Metropole

VCB   Vienna Convention Bureau

WKÖ   Wirtschaftskammer Österreich

WTCA World Trade Center's Association

WTC   World Trade Centers

1. INTRODUCTION

The introduction will present the objectives, the research questions, the methodology, the significance and the delimitation of the diploma thesis.

1.1. Research questions

The author's research questions deal with experienced industry problems as well as general and specific research questions.

1.1.1. Problems:

The problems are focused on the PCO's role evolution, new technologies competition and consumer's choice.

1.1.1.1. The PCO's role evolution

Owing to the rapid development and ferocious competition in the business industry during these last years and considering the fact that congresses are nowadays much more than simply meetings allowing the exchange of information and face to face negotiation, the PCO has become an important way of congress organization and promotion. Obviously the simple fact of providing and assuring good performance and quality in terms of logistics and organization is no longer sufficient.

Nowadays a PCO is involved in a far wider spectrum of activities, including the establishment of goals and objectives, the desired return on investment, as well as the principles of adult learning and successful communication. Other criteria such as guarantees and security and risk management have become important and are indispensable conditions for congress organization. The PCO's role is no longer one of a simple organizer and administrator but also a consultant in many areas. To sum up, the requirements for organizers have evolved during the past years. The capacity to design, plan and adapt to client's requirements such as the late participation, have fast gained importance.

1.1.1.2. Competition

Increment in competition between markets is another problem. The competition is actually the interplay of action and reaction. Suppliers intend to assert a big part of demand by using and playing with different marketing measures such as prices, promotion or product development, which provoke reactions from competitors.

1.1.1.3. New technologies

Thanks to the development of new technology and know-how, the exchange of information is becoming faster and people have to gather together more often to be informed about the latest developments and trends. Thus the business industry including the congress industry is becoming more and more important.

1.1.1.4. Consumer's choice

All destinations share certain characteristics and their success in attracting tourists will depend upon the quality of three essential benefits that they offer to the tourist: attractions, amenities (facilities) and accessibility. Destinations offer service bundles which are consumed by the tourist. When choosing a destination the tourist compares the different areas and their respective service bundles and chooses the one that best fulfils his needs – no matter if this tourist is an individual traveler or a corporation looking for a meeting venue. Thus, a destination has to be managed in a process- and consumer-oriented way, comprising all the levels of the chain of services to be successful in the long-run.

1.1.2. General research question

Regarding the problems mentioned above, this research project aims finding key factors of success for an emerging congress destination, meaning which are today's factors of influence which lead to a successful congress.

1.1.3. Specific research question

This research is trying to point out the weaknesses and strengths regarding their experience, their marketing efforts and image in comparison of both competitive cities Lille and Linz, as well as looking at future perspectives, such as the potential positioning of an emerging congress destination. It is also important to understand which factors promote a destination.

The author will examine the following questions:

> ➢ Is the congress industry an outweigh engine of tourism?

> ➢ Based on which factors do meeting planners and decision makers choose meeting destinations and how can this concept be applied to measuring the attractiveness of meeting destinations?

> ➢ Are emerging destinations a real competitor for congress destinations such as Paris or Vienna?

1.2. Methodology

The study will apply and investigate both primary and secondary data. The author aims at finding answers to questions on how to evaluate the market by means of the "4Ps": price, product, promotion and place as success factors and future trends will also be considered.

The research component of the thesis is obviously based on quantitative and qualitative data, complementing each other; even though the prime data focus has been enlighten on qualitative data. The decision was made to use a qualitative method rather than quantitative methods and helped to make sure that the individuals approached were common with the research topic and representative for the emerging congress destination market.

After having reviewed the research book of Veal, A.J. (2006): Research Methods for Leisure and Tourism, A practical guide and considered the characteristics of the population, the decision was made to send out self-administered questionnaires via e-mail. The author used the survey to be evidence for the keys factors of success and future trends. She assigned the probability that only a limited number of surveys will be received when employing this method. She also wants to mention a crucial element: the survey does not assert one's claims but is a collection of individual perceptions and opinions. Furthermore, the recipients of the questionnaire are professionals and experts having a connection to the business tourism sector.

The dispatch of questionnaires via e-mail allows saving time and money in collecting and processing data. The author could reach more easily the contacts, located not only in Austria or France, but also in Europe and Canada. However, the use of this channel, presented also disadvantages such as the impossibility to offer help and assistance, the low response rate or incomplete questionnaires received. The questionnaires consisted in closed and opened questions. Nevertheless, opened questions were not considered as expert interviews. The surveys were sent out on a regular basis between July and October 2007 as attachments to e-mails informing the recipients about the author's research field and the goal of the work. The questionnaire was sent to 622 professionals. The response rate to the questionnaire was extremely low as expected, so be it, 10.9 % of the recipients answered corresponding to a total of 68 answers.

Due to this low response rate, the survey unfortunately could not be considered as representative. Possible reasons might be that the recipients are until now not familiar with the destinations investigated and did not have related experiences so far. The reasons referred to the lack of knowledge on the respective destinations and complete the general questions or simply because they did not have time to fill in the questionnaire or more that they did not return the survey.

1.2.1. Qualitative research

Figure 1: Coding tree

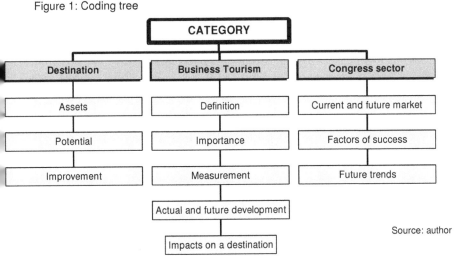

Source: author

This investigation is carried out by means of in-depth face to face interviews with representatives of professional conference organizers professionals and professionals related to business tourism.

Interviewees are quoted to illustrate and maintain their arguments.

1.2.2. Quantitative research

Within the framework of an empirical investigation, the author intends to determine success factors in general: program, marketing and sales, logistic, dates, location/venue, environment, image, attractiveness, competitiveness to find out the importance of the location as a success factor. A survey has been elaborated via Sphynx with the objective to evaluate the following criteria.

- ➤ To organize a congress
- ➤ To select a destination
- ➤ Key factors of success

The data have been examined with Sphynx but graphs and tables created with Excel.

1.3. Significance

This study research could serve to improve the implementation of an emerging congress destination and provide information on how to become an attractive location. The research is in fact a marketing study which could be used by different agencies and organizations to improve their knowledge of emerging congress destination markets. Moreover the research is written in English and could be utilized by any country. The study research also contributes to creating expectations about future markets and to analyzing future trends.

1.4. Limitation

One of the main limitations of the study was the fact that the term congress undifferentiated from the other types of meeting and can be categorized as convention, conference or meeting. The industry is relatively new and booming; that is one of the reasons why specific data do not really exist at the moment. Furthermore congress is not differentiated from the other meetings and usually data provided include all types of meetings existing and are defined under the business tourism idiom. Likewise with the literature, some sub-chapters are dedicated to the congress tourism but not singular books. Another limitation has been the diversity of data in English, German and French languages.

1.5. Delimitation

The topic concerns emerging congress destinations but also introduces the business tourism in general. The study is focused on congress industry and on the two congress destinations of Linz and Lille as emerging congress destinations. It also refers to three dimensions:

> The emergence
> The destination
> The congress sector

The author will consider all these points whilst answering the problem and pointing out the success factors and future trends.

2. NORD - PAS DE CALAIS

Figure 2: Map of the region Nord-Pas-de-Calais

Source: Insee, Comité Régionalde Tourisme Nord - Pas de Calais

Nord-Pas-de-Calais is one of the 26 regions of France and consists of the departments of Nord and Pas-de-Calais, in the north and has a border with Belgium. Until the end of the 20th century both the region and the department were called Nord. The region was once part of the Southern Netherlands, within the Low Countries, and permanently became a part of France in 1713. The historical provinces now included in Nord-Pas-de-Calais are Artois and Flanders, designations which are still frequently used by the inhabitants.

The region of Nord-pas-de-Palais has 2 414 km² representing 2, 3 % of France with 140 km of littoral coasts. It is an extremely densely populated region with some 4 million inhabitants representing around 7% of France's total population, making it the fourth most populous region in France.

The region is ranked 9th place in term of arrival volume and 8th place in overnight stays.

The main tourists are from United Kingdom, Belgium and Germany.

Figure 2: Arrival of foreigners in the hotel industry in 2006

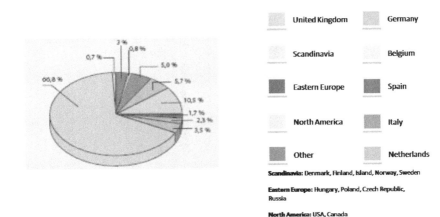

Source: Insee, Comité Régional de Tourisme Nord - Pas de Calais

2.1. The department of Nord

The department attracts more than 2 millions of tourists. The foreign tourists are in majority from Europe, from the neighbor countries such as United Kingdom, Belgium and Netherland.

In term of tourist arrivals the department observed an increase compared to 2005 with a majority of French tourists.

The business tourists display an occupation rate of 68% in the hotel industry.

Figure 3: Hotels occupation rate in 2006

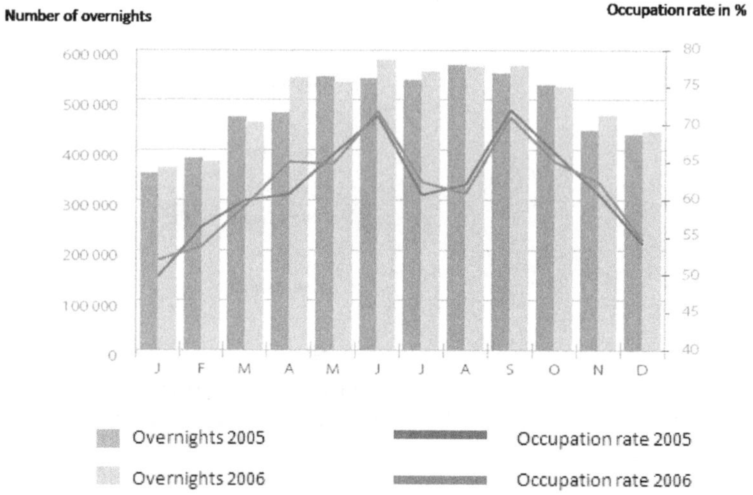

Source : Insee, Comité Régional de Tourisme Nord - Pas de Calais

The most favorite type of accommodation is the bottom end hotel industry

The INSEE (National Institute for Statistics and Economic Studies), Regional Committee of Tourism of Nord-Pas-de-Calais measured the occupation rate of the different hotel category in 2006 and the results are presented as follows:

0 star hotel: 74,4 %

1 star hotel: 63,0 %

2 star hotel: 62,4 %

3 star hotel: 59,2 %

4 star hotel: 55,6%

3. LILLE

Elegant, sophisticated and vibrant, the capital of French Flanders is within easy reach of Calais and is ideal for a day trip or a short break. Lille is also renowned for its shopping and culture; the Fine Arts Museum has an impressive collection and the numerous stores of Lille have a rich diversity of goods, from designer labels and modern shopping malls to unusual boutiques and flea markets. This lively, cosmopolitan city also boasts a bustling café life and a wealth of evening entertainment. The city of Lille is located in the North of France in the region of Nord Pas de Calais and has 220.000 inhabitants. It has the privileged geographical situation in the centre of the Paris - London - Brussels triangle.

Figure 3: City map of Lille

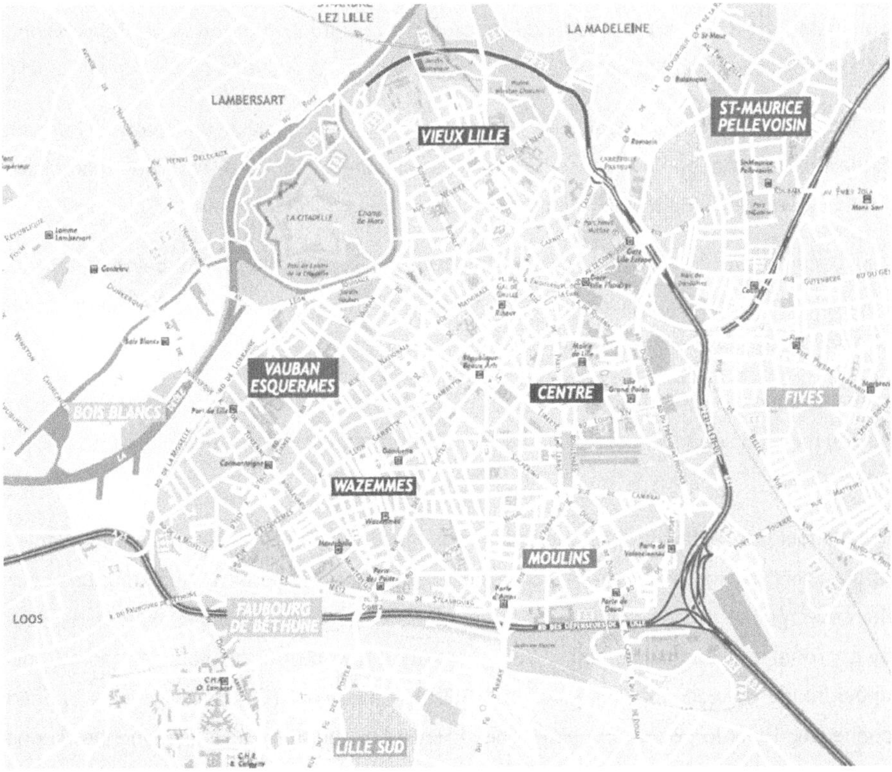

Source: Town Hall of Lille

3.1. History

Lille was born out of the water of the Deûle River, a slow-flowing tributary situated on a major route between the great Flemish towns and the Champagne fairs.

The city was first mentioned in the charter of 1066, in which Baudouin V, Count of Flanders, endowed the Sainte-Pierre collegiate church. In this document the town is called Isla, from the Latin insula literally meaning *island*. Lille was therefore a port initially developed as a transshipment point on the Deûle and leaded Lille to a merchant town.

Countess Jeanne of Flanders governed alone after the battle of Bouvines (1214) and made Lille her primary residence. Lille became part of Burgundy in 1384. This was a time of prosperity for the town. The dukes made it one of their favorite residences, along with Dijon and Brussels. Under their government, Lille was the setting for some magnificent banquets. In 1453, Philippe the Good ordered the construction of the huge Palais Rihour to house his court of 1200 people.

In 1667, Louis XIV conquered Lille during the War of Devolution and passed from the Spanish Netherlands to France. From this starting point, the city was completely transformed and modernized. The current old town was built during the 17th century.

Lille became a great industrial power in the 19th century, its main pillars being metalwork, chemistry and, above all, textiles (cotton and linen).The Revolution saw the rise to power of a liberal, dynamic and entrepreneurial middle class.

Large avenues and vast squares were laid out in the Haussmann style and were the setting for imposing monuments such as the Prefecture, the Palais des Beaux-Arts and the universities.

Throughout the 1960s and 70s, the region was faced with some problems after the decline of the coal, mining and textile industries. Lille entered a period of restructuring based on the development of the service sector. The city of factories and workshops was replaced by one of offices and services. In 1983, the VAL, the world's first automated rapid transit underground network, was opened. In 1993, a high-speed TGV train line was opened, connecting Paris to Lille in one hour. This, followed by the opening of the Channel Tunnel in 1994 and the arrival of the Eurostar train, puts Lille in the centre of a triangle connecting Paris, London, and Brussels.

The creation of the new Euralille district and the arrival of Eurostar in 1994, which lead the city to enter the third millennium: renovation, rejuvenation, reinvention and, re-stimulation.

Today, Lille is the France's fourth largest metropolitan area with international crossroads and a dynamic financial centre and is still the economic centre of the region with new information and communication enterprises springing up alongside the traditional industries.

To enhance and award these changes, the city was chosen as a European Culture Capital in 2004.

Since then, Lille has become an important tourist destination, recognized for its welcoming living environment, well-preserved heritage and active cultural life.

(Source: Lille, Tourist office)

3.2. Access

Lille is qualified as "the easiest European destination to get to", thanks to its modern and varied infrastructure. It also has a dense, modern and fast network of urban transport allowing people to move easily in and around the city. The city has unique connections to the biggest metropolis by:

> ➢ Plane

The Lille-Lesquin international airport located 10 minutes from the town centre and served by a regular shuttle service.

The airport offers day return trips linking more than 60 national and international destinations.

The Lille-Lesquin international airport welcomed more than 1 million of passenger in 2007, corresponding to a growth of 12.7% compared to 2006 by serving over 20 national and international destinations.

National flights service 8 big French metropolises

According to a survey realized in 2004 for analyzing the client's satisfaction, the train stays the most important way of transport to reach the city.

> ➢ Motorways

It is a central hub of 5 motorways: A1 (Paris), A27 (Brussels), A23 (Valenciennes), A25 (Dunkirk, London), A22 (Ghent, Amsterdam), A26 (Lyon).

> ➢ Rail

Lille has 2 stations located directly in the city centre

Lille Flandres Station: TER regional trains and direct TGV service to Paris
Lille Europe Station: Eurostar service to London (reachable in 80 minutes) and Brussels, direct TGV service to Roissy Airport, Paris and all major French cities

TGV connections with big cities such as:

- Lyon, 11 direct connections a day in 3 hours;
- Strasbourg in 3 hours and 20 minutes;
- Marseille 6 direct a day in 4 hours and 30 minutes
- and Bordeaux 6 direct connections a day in 5 hours

Lille is also located less than an hour away by train from the two international airports: Paris Charles de Gaulle in 51 minutes, TGV direct connections a day, Brussels Zaventem in 38 minutes, providing 14 Eurostar train connections a day.

> ➢ Waterways

Lille is the third largest French river port after Paris and Strasbourg.

The river Deûle is connected to regional waterways with over 680 km of navigable waters. The Deûle connects to Northern Europe via the River Scarpe and the River Escaut (towards Belgium and the Netherlands), and internationally via the Lys (to Dunkerque and Calais).

> ➢ Urban public transport connections
>   - 2 metro lines, (Lille- Regional Hospital Centre – Villeneuve d'Ascq 4 Cantons/ Tourcoing Hospital Centre Dron – Lomme Saint Philibert Hospital): 60 stations, 45 km.
>   - 2 tramway lines, (Lille-Roubaix/Lille-Tourcoing): 36 stations, 19 km.
>   - 45 bus lines.
> ➢ Parking facilities

Lille has street level car parks offering about 20,000 parking spaces, metro car parks in the city centre and on-street pay-and-display ticket parking.

(Source: Lille, Tourist office)

3.3. Economy

The city of Lille had two associated localities the town of Hellemmes since 1977 and Lomme since 2000.

The economic dynamism of Lille is meant by its 4 out of 6 of the poles of competitiveness in the Nord-Pas-de-Calais region: Up-Tex (textiles), Nutrition-Health-Longevity, industries of commerce and materials for domestic use.

The attraction of the Lille area in terms of economic inward investment is favored by the availability of prime real estate potential in the form of dedicated business parks specialized according to different economic sectors. Lille counts nowadays 8,341 businesses, whose 8, 86% are industry, 33,92% commerce and 57,22% services.

For example, the centrally situated Euralille welcomes tertiary businesses, whereas Eurasanté is dedicated to the healthcare sector and, finally, Euratechnologies is a new pole of excellence in the domain of the latest technologies.

3.3.1. Lille Metropole

The Urban Community of Lille Metropole (Lille Métropole Communauté Urbaine - LMCU) is a public body forming the basis for intercommunity cooperation created in 1967. The UCLM brings together 85 towns within a territory which has both urban and rural parts. The main goals of UCLM were concerned initially with urban planning issues and public service provision, but have evolved since new legislation in July 1999 to extend in addition the links between the constituent communes. The actual President of the Urban Community of Lille Metropole is former French Prime Minister, Pierre Mauroy. It has become the key public stakeholder in the urban regeneration process.

The conurbation was the base for much heavy manufacturing in the nineteenth and early twentieth century's, particularly in the wool and cotton industries. To face unattractive areas such as the former industrial sites turned into derelict wastelands, Lille Metropole has evolved its approach to regeneration over many years into a twin track policy of promoting individual image-enhancing schemes ('unifying projects') alongside wholesale urban regeneration of large defined areas (often central areas) based on grand partnerships of national, regional, local and private stakeholders. This dual approach has developed largely as a result of particular events and trends.

Lille Metropole is the 15th European metropole, first European transborder city and is in the heart of European's richest and most dynamical area, so be it 1 million consumers in a radius of 300 kilometers. It has 84 kilometers of common border with Belgium and forms with Courtrai, Mouscron, Roselaere, Tournai and Ypres urban districts an important cross boarding built-up area. It also homes a total of 43,923 industrial and commercial businesses including 3,890 industries, 3,364 wholesale trade, 12,590 retail and repair trade, 24,079 services.

Lille Metropole is

> ➢ A major international trade centre with 2,000 exporters and 3,000 importers.
> ➢ A high-performance logistics hub thanks to the presence of major names in domestic and international logistics, European logistics centers (Lille Airport, Lille Port, Lille Lesquin Regional Transport Centre...) and major regional distribution groups

> 5 competitive clusters, including 1 with an international role, strengthening links between companies, research units and training centers based around innovative projects: I-TRANS (Rail at the heart of innovative transport systems), UP-TEX (High-performance textile), Nutrition Health Longevity (Innovation in food and health), Commerce Industries (Laboratory for commerce of the future), and MAUD (Materials for Domestic Use).

> 5 centers of excellence devoted to leading edge technologies: EURALILLE I and II (Tertiary), EURASANTE (Bio Park), HAUTE BORNE (Technologies and Innovation), EURATECHNOLOGIES (ICT), L'UNION (Innovative textiles, Image and Distribution).

> 15 international company headquarters: 3 Suisses International, Arc International, Auchan, Barco, Beaulieu Wielsbeke, Bekaert, Bonduelle, Cofidis, Décathlon, Finaref, Leroy Merlin, Lesaffre, Picañol, Redcats, Roquette.

> Europe's no.1 hub for mail order and distance selling.

> France's no.1 centre for the textile industry.

> France's second centre for the printing and publishing industry, and for the insurance industry.

> France's third largest centre for the engineering and electronics industry, food-processing industry, financial services including consumer credit, and the chemical, pharmaceutical and health industries.

> France's third largest office market with 114,000 m² of office space marketed in 2005. (Source: http://www.lillemetropole.fr/ and www.destination-lille-metropole.eu)

3.3.2. Euralille

Euralille was at the beginning an urban remodeling project which began in 1991. The decision to build such a complex was taken by Pierre Mauroy, mayor of the city at that time and ex-Prime Minister from 1981 to 1984. He wanted to develop a big project around the future TGV station to accompany the development of the service sector. The Euralille Centre was opened in 1994. However, the Euralille urban development project, centered on the new TGV station has fostered a long debate among Lille's citizens. The project has finally been completed with modern architecture and disruption to the ancient city centre.

Euralille is the current business centre, the third in France after -La Défense- and -Le Part-Dieu- and is spread on 110 hectares with remodeled district is now full of parks and modern buildings containing offices, shops, and apartments. In 1994 the Grand Palais was also opened.

The program covers 310 000 m² of office space, 100 000 m² of activities and stores, 45 000 m² of hotels, 178 000 m² of accommodation, 110 000 m² of public facilities, 6 000 parking places and 15 hectares of green space, effectively underscoring the fact that Euralille is by no means a mere «business district». The complex homes:

> ➢ The two stations: Lille Flanders and Lille Europe
> ➢ A shopping centre representing 66.000 m² selling area including
> ➢ A hypermarket of 10.000 m² and 120 shops towers of "Crédit Lyonnais" bank, Lille Europe, Atrium, business city and Eurocity recovering a total 81.000 m²
> ➢ NIIP, National Institute of Industrial Property
> ➢ The Henri Matisse urban Park (Source: http://www.saem-euralille.fr/)

3.3.3. Eurasanté

Eurasanté is an agency specialized in the economic development of the health sector of the Lille Nord-Pas de Calais Region.

The agency aims to create jobs and adds new competences in the field of biohealth at the regional   level
as well as to develop the Lille Nord Pas-de-Calais Health Pole
It ensures all activities linked to economic development by enhancing the know-how of health   professionals

and assisting local companies and organize an international promotion of the Regional Biohealth Pole and of the Eurasanté Park by assisting in the installation of foreign companies within the Lille Nord Pas-de-Calais Health Pole. (Source: http://www.eurasante.com/)

3.3.4. Euratechnologies

This is a pole dedicated to the NTIC and covering an area of 100 hectares.

Two industrial buildings Plan – Lafont are renovated to home office space and have been opened since 2007 and represent 23.000 m² of net floor area and will realize a Global Internet Exchange (GIX). Estimations about employments at the moment figure up to 1.000. But in a very close future, the project intends to increase this surface of 150.000 m² of net floor area and create 3.000 new jobs. 170 000 m² of net floor area for accommodations will be erected, so be it corresponding to 1.800 tenements welcoming around 4.000 inhabitants. The project should be completed in 2012. (Source: http://www.lillemetropole.fr/index.php?p=429&art_id=11725)

3.3.5. Chamber of commerce and industry of Grand Lille

The creation Chamber of Commerce and Industry, uniting the chamber of Commerce and Industry of Armentières Hazebrouck, Douai, Lille Métropole and Saint-Omer Saint-Pol, was issued in the official journal on May, 8th 2007. The Chamber of Commerce and Industry of Grand Lille officially installed its head office in the centre of Lille in December 2007. (Source: http://www.grand-lille.cci.fr/). The CCI Grand Lille is the fifth CCI of France (behind Paris, Versailles, Marseille and Lyon) with 61.000 businesses as per following split:

Table 1: Dispersion of the businesses

Sectors	CCI Grand Lille
Industry	5.510 (9,1%)
Construction	5.268 (8,7%)
Services	32.394 (53,5%)
Commerce	17.378 (28,7%)

Source: INSEE

3.4. Tourism

"Lille is a trendy destination" (Mrs. Vitel ,CCI Lille, see p.VI)

These last years, Lille has become an important tourist and cultural destination. Indeed the city has been named Cultural Capital of Europe since 2004 and also Art and History city. Moreover it owns the -Palais des Beaux-Arts- Museum which is the second most visited museum after -Le Louvre-. The city is also reputed for its warm welcome and conviviality. Lille is a short break destination; most of the tourists stay less than 4 nights. Designated as the European Capital of Culture in 2004, Lille today meets the expectations of economic decision-makers and attracts increasing numbers of tourists. Indeed, Lille is becoming more and more established as a tourist destination. The vibrancy of Lille 2004 European Capital of Culture and many other cultural events, such as those organized on the theme of India as part of the Lille 3000 festival, demonstrate the youthful "joie de vivre" of the city. Two promotion actions are lead at the moment:

➢ On the leisure tourism by participating in professional and general public trade shows and being attentive that Lille is programmed in French Tour-Operator.

➢ On the event tourism by attracting new customers and creating the organization of a festival with international recognition.

3.4.1. Tourist office

As a non-profit association, the Tourist office is a precious tool for Lille's tourist development policy. The town council entrusts the office with the mission to welcome and inform visitors and to promote the town as a tourist destination. Furthermore, as an active partner in the town's policy to develop and promote its heritage, the board commercializes tours organized by guide-lecturers for whom it is responsible, in close partnership with the Town Council. The tourist office receives in the mean 4 to 500.000 tourists.

60% are foreigners of which 1 out of 2 are from Great Britain and 1 in 3 from Belgium. German, Dutch, American and Canadian tourists also visit the city.

40% come from France, with the majority of people coming from the region of Paris. (Source: Masson, C., Tourist Office, see p.VI)

3.5. Offer

3.5.1. Accommodation and Gastronomy

In 2003, Lille recorded 16.000 beds in 246 places of accommodation.

The hotel business is pointed on a second scale by a majority (37% are two-star hotels). Nevertheless the city possesses the 10th hotel park of France with an annual occupancy rate of 65% in 2006.

Occupation rate by category in 2006:

> ➢ 0-1 star hotel: 73,3 %
> ➢ 0-2 star hotel: 63,9%
> ➢ 3 star hotel: 67,7 %
> ➢ 4 star hotel: 61,6%

(Source: Regional Committee of Nord-pas-de-Calais)

Rates remain stable, except for independent hotels, which have been increased up to 20% between 2004 and 2007. This allowed renovating and improving the hotel quality.

3.5.1.1. The Hotelier Club

The Hotelier Club association was created in 1988. It aims to federate hotels to improve the clients' reception, the hotel business quality and relations with institutions. It is composed of more than 60 members with more than 4.300 rooms in Lille Metropole, representing 85% of the hotel park. Two-thirds of the members are independent hotels and the rest, are hotel chains. The association has taken an active part in creating the Meeting Guide.

3.5.1.2. The -Tables Gourmandes- Club

In 1999, a handful of restaurant owners from greater Lille decided to join forces and create the -Tables Gourmandes- Club, backed by the CCI. 25 very different institutions based throughout the greater Lille, from Seclin to Marcq-en-Baroeul by way of Bondues and Lille, are members of this club. This club, a real fusion of culinary talents, works towards the promotion of regional gastronomy - carbonade, potjevleesch, as well as national cuisine, thanks to active members who wants to make their establishments "alive" as well as their kitchens.

3.5.2. Shopping facilities

Lille has a great variety of shops and businesses, from small local stores to major international names, including the arrival of the Galeries Lafayette in new 13,000 m² premises in the pedestrians city centre in 2007. According to Mr. Masson (tourist office, see p.VI), the shopping facility is one of the main attraction reason of the target group from Paris and surroundings. The city offers almost the same ensigns than in Paris except that the city is at a human scale size and everything can be done afoot. (Source: Tourist Office)

3.5.3. City pass: 1,2, 3 days

The city facilitates moves inside and outside Lille thanks to the city pass created by the tourist office and the tourist promotion funds. Lille is therefore positioned as the entrance door of the region Nord-pas-de-Calais. It is composed of a check system and allows tourists to get discounts on certain museum entrances and exhibitions, transport fees, etc Partners programming the destination are more and more interested and willing to sell the city pass in a package.

3.5.4. Congress Pass:

It was created on the same example as the city pass. It costs € 2, and provides unlimited access to the Transpole network for the whole period of the congress.

3.5.5. City-break and week-end packages

Theme and event packages are put in place to attract this kind of clients. These comprises for example:

Theme packages: Well-being package, Lille romantic holiday or on the event of the Christmas market, the Braderie, etc

Mr. Masson (Tourist office, see p.VI) draws up the typology of the customers as persons with a definite buying power, without children and travelling.

3.5.6. Guiding services and City tour

The City Tour is a minibus going all around the city available 7 days a week and offers the tour in 8 languages. The city also invites tourists to discover Lille with an Allovisit audio guide indicating how to get from site to site. It even suggests shortcuts. The service is available 7 days a week, 24 hours a day. 7 stages, about 3 minutes each:

> Palais Rihour
> Grand'Place
> Place du Théâtre
> Rue Grande Chaussée
> Hospice Comtesse
> Cathédrale Notre-Dame de la Treille
> Rue Esquermoise.

3.6. Culture

"Lille, European capital of culture in 2004 allowed the city to gain 10 years of image in advance" (Mr. Masson, tourist office, see p. VI)

Lille more than all other destinations in France wants to give access to the culture and popularize it. Beyond, an effort for international customers is done by translating exhibitions in English or Dutch. The rich architectural heritage of the city, its cultural diversity and festive atmosphere (including the great –Braderie- flea-market held on the first weekend each September) are among the reasons bringing many visitors from across France and abroad. The most visited and appreciated monuments are Euralille and Lille's Fine Arts Museum -Palais des Beaux Arts- second largest in France, after the Louvre and the old city centre.

3.6.1. Fine Arts Museum

The museum was restored in 1997. From a previous 15,000 m2, the museum's surface area was increased to 22,000 m2, as the basements were converted into halls for the mediaeval and Renaissance collections. It also includes a hall for temporary exhibitions, an auditorium, a library and a space devoted to pedagogical workshops. The collections of the -Palais des Beaux-Arts- comprise worldwide renowned objects and provide a comprehensive panorama of the great artistic movements of Europe from the 12th to the 20th century. The museums had 233.000 visitors in 2005.

3.6.2. -The Braderie-

-The Braderie- is a 48 hour festival of second-hand goods dealers all around the city of Lille which occurs every first weekend in September. It is a tradition from the middle Ages, when once a year the servant classes of Lille were given permission to sell – from dusk to dawn – old clothes and objects belonging to their employers.

3.7. Labels

3.7.1. The Art and Historic City

Classified as a city of "Art et Histoire" since 2004, the department coordinates and implements initiatives within the framework of the «Art and Historic City» program. (Source: http://www.mairie-lille.fr/sections/site-en/A_la_une/discover-tale-citadel)

3.7.2. Towns and regions of art and history network

The Ministry for Culture's architecture and heritage directorate grants the label, -villes et pays d'art et d'histoire- to local authorities committed to revitalizing their heritage. It guarantees the proficiency of architecture and heritage guide-lecturers and coordinators, together with the quality of the activities they propose. From antique vestiges to 20th Century architecture, Cities and Regions of art and history put the great diversity of their heritage on show. Today, the network includes 126 towns and regions. (Source: http://www.mairie-lille.fr/sections/site-en/A_la_une/discover-tale-citadel)

4. BUSINESS TOURISM IN LILLE

The fact that Lille tried to organize the Games of the XXVIIIth Olympiad in 2004 has led up to positioning the city on a European and international level not only for tourism and business tourism but also in terms of image and brand. In 2003 the business clients represented 62.9% of the hotel activity.

4.1. Congress activity

The city hosts national and international congresses and announces 55, 3 billion Euro of turnover for an average of 8 fairs organized relating to the textile and mail orders activities.

4.2. Lille Event's Club

The club was created five years ago and gathers together tourist providers such as welcoming agencies, restaurants, night clubs and transport companies, etc with the goal of sell the image of Lille. Thus, 37 partners have put in common their know-how to bring to organizers the best quality service. (Source: Press release Lille Métropole, une destination de tourisme d'affaires en plein essor, 2004)

4.3. Lille Meeting Guide

Due to the business tourism boom, three actors of Lille Metropole, the –Hotelier Club, - Tables Gourmandes- Club and the -Lille Events'- Club were regrouped in coordination with the tourist office and the Chamber of Commerce and Industry to create the -Meeting Guide-, first published in February, 2004. This guide aims to help events' organizers by referencing all business tourism professionals in Lille Metropole. The guide also presents the destination of Lille Metropole as a whole. The meeting guide is the instrument of the convention bureau. (Source: Press release Lille Métropole, une destination de tourisme d'affaires en plein essor, 2004)

4.4. Structures in charge of the congress activity

The following points will present the different organizations and associations related to the business tourism.

4.4.1. World Trade Centre

Founded in 1970 in New York, the World Trade Center's Association (WTCA) is today a powerful global network of 300 business centers distributed over the 5 continents. Its mission is to strengthen international relations by facilitating exchanges and creating and developing the World Trade Centers throughout the world. Each WTC is an independent organization offering products and customized services to facilitate and strengthen the presence of a company nationally or its international development. It is also a privileged hosting place bringing together the economic players around unifying themes thus promoting encounter and exchange. The Lille World Trade Centre is a development player and a platform for exchange and gives access to:

➤ Business centre services: translation, interpreting, domiciliation, hiring of rooms
➤ Business clubs to develop your own business network
➤ International business networks and their high involvement in the economic life of the region.

The WTC of Lille homed in 2007:

➤ 12 foreign delegations
➤ 27 information meetings
➤ 1.000 participants and 30,000 visitors

It aims to:

➤ Bring businesspeople into contact with each other and promote new projects
➤ Promote member's activities
➤ Improve the international profile of the region of Lille
➤ Enhance the impact of WTCA network (http://www.wtc-lille.org/uk_sommaire.php)

4.4.2. Congress centre-Lille Grand Palais

The following item is going to present the Grand Palais, its components and its activities.

4.4.2.1. Facts and figures

Like many cities in France, Lille has its own congress centre: -Lille Grand Palais-, built in 1994. The building has a tri-modal design of: conferences, exhibitions and and zenith modules which are interconnected and complement each another, unique in Europe. Furthermore they are combined with all the technological equipment. It holds 3 exposition halls with a square area of 18.000 m² including 3 amphitheatres, 16 rooms as well as banquets, press and VIP spaces. It contributes to make Lille Grand Palais a functional, aesthetic and versatile complex. With 22, 000 m² of exhibition space, 3 amphitheatres, 16 committee rooms and the Zenith offering a capacity from 2.000 to 7.000 places, Lille Grand Palais can be adapted to any type of event attended by between 10 and 50.000 people and providing at the same time a maximum of comfort and optimum flow management. The congress centre is one of the 5 most important congress centers in France, attracting over 1 million visitors and listing 9 million Euros as well as a minimum of 125,000 overnight stays per year. Lille Grand Palais works in close collaboration with Eurasanté, the Minister institute and the CHR. (Source: Lille Grand Palais)

Its objective is to obtain the sponsoring of important people of the region and attract congresses specialized in Lille (the medical and scientific sector being one of the biggest users of congress in the world). Lille Grand Palais weaves links always closer and closer with all the local partners as well as with the professionals of the event and the business tourism, by federating them around the same ambition, to make Lille Metropole an inescapable meeting for event' organizers. In addition, Lille Grand Palais contributes to the attractiveness of Lille and its region. The Grand Palais has financial amounting to more than 2 million Euro support from:

> City of Lille: 61.7%
> Chamber of Commerce: 7.1%
> Tourist Office: 0.001%
> GL Event: 8.1%
> Crédit Mutuel of Nord Europe Bank: 8.5%
> Scalbert Dupont Bank: 4.8%
> Caisse d'Epargne Nord Europe: 4.8%

> Dalkia: 4.7%

Table 2: Balance sheet activities 2006-2007

Total displays	310
- corporate events	103
- congresses	82
- exhibitions	43
- zenith	82
Number of visitors	1.035.724
- congresses	148.792
- exhibitions	503.950
- zenith	382.982
Origin of visitors	
- regional	62%
- national	23%
- international	15%
Turnover	12.752.546 Euro
net profit*	474.755 (so be it, 3.72% of the turnover)
* Unsubsidized, after payment of a rent in the City of Lille	
Turnover by activities	
- association and corporate	5.2 million Euro
- exhibition	3.6 million Euro
- production	1.4 million Euro
- show	2.5 million Euro

Source: Press release Lille Grand Palais, December 2007, Djamila Vandenberghe

Table 3: Direct, indirect and induced economic impacts

Number of visitors	1.035.724 Euro
Direct economic impacts (costs of staff + local tax system + consumption + investments)	12.733.600 Euro

Indirect economic impacts
 	
(Measure the expenses of congress participants, visitors or spectators to local providers.)
 	
Overnights
  - Hotels
  - Restaurants
  - Shops and services
  - Transport / parking
	23.516.431 Euro
	
	122.759 Euro
	12.275.932 Euro
	6.221.816 Euro
	3.006.269 Euro
	1.889.655 Euro

Induced economic impacts	52.032.271 Euro
Total	88.159.543 Euro

Source: Press release Lille Grand Palais, December 2007, Djamila Vandenberghe

4.4.2.2. Congress area

The congress sector includes:

> ➢ 3 auditoriums: Vauban (1 500 places), Pasteur (500 places) and Eurotop (300 places) all equipped with audiovisual broadcasting: simultaneous translation, video, projection rooms and professional state control.
> ➢ 27 rooms of committees on 4 levels (from 10 to 400 places) and a flexible general-purpose space (400 divisible places).
> ➢ The Flanders space of 1 650 m² (400 places or twice 200 places).
> ➢ The set is equipped in simultaneous translation.
> ➢ The Business space (up to 125 sitting places).

At the same time place of work and relaxation, the privative, comfortable and functional space, benefits from complete multimedia equipment.

4.4.2.3. Activity

Regarding its activity, 75% of visitors are Franco-French and 25% international. 5 to 6 international congresses with a world scale are organized each year.

Figure 3: The activity of the Lille Grand Palais

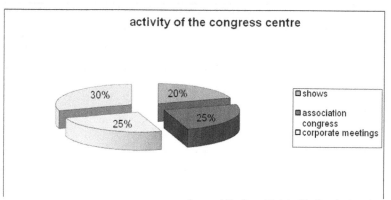

Source: Lille Grand Palais, Mr. Caucheteux (see p.V)

The congress centre differentiates itself from other congress centers by the mean that only few others combine a show area and exhibition area.

The congress centre homes 310 displays between July, 2006 and June, 2007, corresponding to an occupation rate of 85% and a turnover of more than 10 billion Euro, ranking the congress centre to the third place after the congress centers of Paris and Lyon.

4.4.3. Chamber of Commerce and Industry (CCI) – Mrs. Vitel (see p.VI)

Mrs. Vitel, in charge of the tourism-events-congress department works together with the Convention Bureau and the congress center.

4.4.4. Convention bureau – Mr. Charles –Eric Vilain XIIII (see p. VI)

The Convention Bureau has been created in July, 2006 but is effective since January, 2007. The activity of Lille Convention Bureau is implementing little by little its strategy and does not yet have all tools to measure the impact of the business tourism.

4.4.4.1. Files negotiated in 2007

125 files negotiated so be it a total of 2 111 700 Euros (calculation according to the number of persons and overnights).

Table 4: Contracts negotiated in 2007

Files confirmed	Files in process	Files lost	Files not proceed
26,4%	20,8%	26,4%	26,4%

Source: Lille Convention Bureau, Dossier de Presse - Janvier 2008 Karen Grand

Table 5: Number of participants (based on a total of 5.142 participants)

0>50	50>100	100 >250	250 >500	500+
27,27%	24,24%	18,18%	18,18%	12,12%

Source: Lille Convention Bureau, Dossier de Presse - Janvier 2008 Karen Grand

Table 6: Number of days (based on a total of 57 days):

1	2	3 et +
54,56%	21,26%	24,24%

Source: Lille Convention Bureau, Dossier de Presse - Janvier 2008 Karen Grand

Table 7: Reasons of files lost (based on a total of 30 files lost)

No more hotel availabilities	Lack of hotels capacity	Late reply from the providers	Incentive non pertinent
30%	20%	48%	2%

Source: Lille Convention Bureau, Dossier de Presse - Janvier 2008 Karen Grand

4.5. SWOT ANALYSIS

Strengths	Weaknesses
• Architecture • Welcoming attitude • Population young: one fourth is less than 25 years old, more than 100.000 students • Dynamism • Great location centre of a triangle connecting Paris, London, and Brussels. • Rail and air connections with European capitals and metropolis • Shopping facilities • One of the most large metropolis in France • European leader of the mail order and the volume retailing such as La Redoute, les 3 Suisses, Auchan; second rank for insurance sector and third	• Lack of urban road signs • Problems of parking areas • Traffic sometimes difficult due to the road renovations... • From January 2008, prohibition to smoke in public areas in France • Lack of hotels and hotels with large capacity (more than 150 rooms) • No hotel chains • Lack of infrastructures to welcome meetings outside Lille Grand Palais • Parking facilities • Image weakness • Promotion • Airport with a national vocation

	No tourism observer
rank for the financial sector • City on a human scale • Good price and quality relation • Gastronomy • Meetings from 50 to 1.000 persons representing 80% of the market 88.000 hectares designated to the agriculture or green areas	
Threats • National competition even more stronger with cities such as Lyon , Marseille, Biarritz and Nice and international competition with cities such as Edinburgh, Dublin, Brussels, Genève, Lisbon, Florence, Copenhagen and Stockholm. • High competition from Eastern and Central countries which invest enormously	**Opportunities** • TGV train allow to easy reach of the city • Being a destination with a change of scene for tourists • Increase in number of shuttles • Important international conference centre • Development of a marketing politic oriented to international congresses • Lille 3000 strength the image of a cultural capital • Importance of the corporate market • Encourage business tourists to extend their stay • Attract more leisure tourists • Internationalization of the airport • Development of a low cost connection

4.5.1. Development of the city – recommendations

- ➤ Positioning of the image as a unique and different brand
- ➤ Increase communication
- ➤ Modernize the infrastructure and improve and install new technology equipments
- ➤ Develop promotion activities to improve the efficiency through a better planning and inclusion in the budget
- ➤ Organize marketing strategies positioned on the association and corporate segment
- ➤ Define the foreign priority markets and put in place of appropriate means
- ➤ Establish a long perspective marketing plan (1,3 and 5 years)

(Source: Lille Metropole Europe Convention Bureau-Strategic Marketing Plan, Mr. Vilain, see p. VI)

5. BUSINESS INDUSTRY IN AUSTRIA

This chapter will describe the key factors of attractiveness of Austria as well as the organizations involved in the business tourism area.

Figure 4: Map of Austria

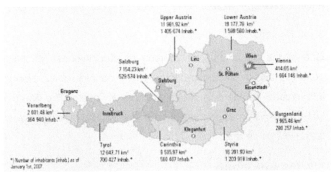

Source: Statistics Austria (doc-Austria data facts and figures 029252)

5.1 Reasons of competitiveness and attractiveness of Austria

Austria has become one of the leaders in the business tourism industry.

5.1.1. Location

Austria benefits of a privileged location, at the heart of Europe, at the intersection between Central and Eastern Europe.

5.1.2. Accessibility

The Austrian Airlines Group (Austrian, Austrian Arrows and Lauda Air) and more than 200 international airlines operate from and to 6 Austrian airports. Concerning the railway, the Austrian railway network is connected to the entire European railway network and qualifies as comfortable, reliable and fast. Furthermore Austria has an excellent motorway infrastructure linking Austria to its neighboring states.

5.1.3. Economic

In terms of economy, Austria is a member of the Economic and Monetary Union of the European Community holding the common currency Euro. The country has shown a stable economic climate and a low inflation rate. Nowadays it is the seat of numerous international organizations such as UNOV, IAEA and UNIDO and attracts even more multinational companies.

5.1.4. Security

One of the most important criteria of attractiveness of Austria is maybe its political neutrality and social policy. Indeed, the country ranks among the top countries in an international comparison of standards/quality of life (The World of 2005-Index of Quality of Life-Economist Intelligence Unit) and economical stability (few strikes, low inflation), along with a low crime rate.

5.2. Infrastructure

In terms of infrastructure, the country offers multifunctional conference centers and distinguished hotels from international luxury hotels to traditional family-owned establishments making the destination one of the most competitive and attractive. Indeed, Austria is home to 19 congress centers and 28 050 places and it also has a modern technical infrastructure with an outstanding congress infrastructure.

5.3. Culture and environment

Austria owns an incredible cultural heritage, symbolized by Vienna. During the 17th and 18th centuries, Austria was one of the major centers of the cultural renaissance: Baroque and The Enlightenment. The country also has homed famous composers, psychologists, philosophers and artists such as Mozart, Klimt, Schiele, Schubert, Rilke, Schnitzler, Freud, Husserl, etc. At the same time, Austria has become a hothouse of striking contemporary architecture, always at the forefront of engineering, invention and design, and with a modern, efficient social system. Austria is proud of its majestic Alps, plentiful forests, 88 lakes and considerable network of rivers. Furthermore, the country is focused on environment protection and its preservation is one of the main goals of the government.

5.4. Business Tourism

"Conferences, corporate meetings and incentives play an important part in Vienna's tourist industry, and account for almost 12% of all overnight stays. Outstanding conference facilities, excellent conference support services and cultural appeal help ensure that Vienna ranks among the leading destinations for international meetings." (Vienna Convention Bureau)

Statistics Austria found out and published the following results about the business and official trips in 2006:

Altogether 4.59 million business and official trips were undertaken. The strongest business trip months in 2006 were Octobers and March (11.6% or 10.7% of annual interest), as well as May (10.0%). Just over half of the business trips (51.4%) took place abroad; and 78.2% of the business and official trips did not last longer than 3 days.

Altogether 1.22 million residents and native citizens (older than 15 years) in the run of 2006 undertook at least one official travel or business trip inland or abroad, representing 17,8% of business trips. Citizens travelling the most (29.5%) are the category of -35-to 44-year-olds.

83, 1 % of business travelers were accommodated in a hotel and 53,3% travelled by car.

5.4.1. Congress Tourism

"Congress tourism is the royal discipline of tourism" (Josef Burger, member of the AUA Managing Board).

Approximately 82% of the congresses held in Austria take place in Vienna, including an average of 13% international congresses in Vienna's main congress centers (RX Messe Wien Congress Center, Austria Center Vienna and the Hofburg), 23% in the universities and 20% in hotels. Vienna continues to hold its leading position in global conference tourism. The Austrian capital is one of the most popular congress cities in the world and ranks in first and second place, respectively, in the two most important international expert rankings. Thanks to Vienna, Austria has moved up to fifth place in the country ranking.

Other advantages of the country are its creative offers and successful management of events through professional Austrian suppliers and various event locations. Tourist expertise qualifies Austrian suppliers for their professionalism, reliability, flexibility and customer-oriented hospitality. Moreover the destination provides optimal price-performance ratio. Other criteria making the country attractive are its optimal accessibility, the state of the art infrastructure and the quality of its services. Austria is one of the Top 10 destinations in international congress tourism and Vienna is one of the top five conference cities of the world. Indeed according to the ICCA statistics in 2006, Austria is ranked in the eighth place (France in fourth) and the first place for Vienna (followed by Paris). Whereas, according to the Brussels-based Union of International Associations (UIA) Statistics for the same year, Austria is ranked in fifth place (and France in the second place) and Vienna in the second place (Paris in the first place).

5.4.2. Structure organizations of the congress

This subdivision is going to explain the different Austrian associations involved in the congress industry.

5.4.2.1. Austrian Business and Convention Network (ACBN)
  ➢ Functions of the ABCN

The ABCN is a non-profit organization, a platform for congresses and conventions and plays the role of an umbrella organization for the whole country. ACBN is a lobbying of the Austrian congress industry and intends to promote, represent as well as to strengthen and expand the position of the country as a congress destination all over the world. It provides services to its members located inland and abroad. Besides its commercial use, it is also primarily a platform for generating new networks, initiating business deals and reinforcing existing customer relations by:

- Increasing the significance of the destination
- Raising the awareness
- Being focalized on the market activities

The ABCN offers the opportunity to generate new buyer classes and, as a one-stop shopping approach, to be a sales generator itself as trade fair. As tourist platform in Central Europe, the ABCN also sets a clear signal for cross-regional cooperation. It is also a tourist market place, industry meeting point and impulse setter.

> Objectives of the ABCN
  - Increase the volume international businesses
  - Promote the attraction of the destination
  - Improve the image of Austria
  - To engage in joint marketing activities in this sector
  - To increase the awareness of the political authorities and decision making bodies (Source: http://www.abcn.at/)

5.4.2.2. Vienna Convention Bureau (VCB)

The VCB was set up in 1969 and is one of the four departments within the Vienna Tourist Board. The tourist board is established as an independent institution and is guaranteed a voice on any issues affecting tourism within the city. The bureau is subsidized by the Vienna City Council and the Vienna Chamber of Commerce. Additional funding comes from sponsors. The VCB is member of different international meeting organizations & associations succh as:

- ASAE - American Society of Association Executives
- DOME - Data on Meetings and Events
- ECM - European Cities Marketing
- DMAI - Destination Marketing Association International
- ICCA - International Congress & Convention Association
- MPI - Meeting Professionals International
- UIA – Union of International Associations

(Source: Vienna Convention Bureau)

6. UPPER AUSTRIA

This chapter is going to enlighten concisely Upper Austria through its culture and tourism activities and will give some information about the business tourism in the province.

Figure 5: Map of Upper Austria

Source : DRIS (Digitales Oberösterreichisches Raum Informations System)

6.1. Facts and figures

Upper Austria has 1.377 million inhabitants, representing 17% of the Austrian population and is the third populous federal region.

The region is managed by a parliament with 56 members and a government with a total of 9 members under the presidency of the minister-president. It is formed of 15 districts and 445 municipalities. The three statutory cities are Linz, Wels and Steyr. Upper Austria was moved back from the edge to the heart of Europe due to the European Union. Furthermore, the region, thanks to its position in the heart of Europe and the River Danube has established various boat connections with countries from Central and East Europe. Upper Austria is also renowned for its dynamic economy. Its trade and industry is based upon five strong columns: salt, iron, agriculture, technology and tourism.

One of the main economic factors in the hill region to the north is agriculture, but this is also Austria´s second most important source of oil and natural gas. The region around the provincial capital, Linz with its modern Danube port installations, is a major centre for the production of iron, steel (Voest-Alpine Steel Group) and chemicals. Other important industrial sectors include vehicle manufacturing in Steyr and the mining and processing of salt in Hallstatt, Bad Ischl and Ebensee. Moreover, Upper Austria is a major tourism centre.

The region has conserved and developed a strong competition and importance in the Industry, Export and Technology activities. Export activities for example provide 26 per cent of total national exports. In fact, export is not only representing an economical strength, but it also leads Upper Austria to the stage of the lowest unemployment rate within the Austrian regions.

In addition to this, Upper Austria is presented as a preserved area. The region emphasizes the energy sector and is on the way of realizing the Kyoto targets to achieve sustainability in all areas not only in the environmental but also in energy politics. More than 30 per cent of the total primary energy consumption is produced from renewable energy sources. Linz, the capital city, is one of the cleanest industrial cities in Europe.

6.2. Culture

Being an intersection of important European traffic routes, the area of Linz has developed to the strong economical and cultural heart of Upper Austria.

Upper Austria is famous for its festivals, numerous expositions all year round as well as diverse and ambitious cultural activities. The region has established an international reputation due to its extensive cultural life and cross-border cultural co-operations, e.g. the -Landesausstellung 2004-, or the -Stifterjahr 2005-. The ordination will be the nomination of Linz as-European capital of culture 2009-.

Around 150 million Euros are spent by the Upper Austrian people for "cultural consumption" each year, making culture an important economic factor in Upper Austria.

6.3. Tourism

The hospitality of the people, the impressive landscapes and the cultural jewels characterize Upper Austria. The Province offers more than 2,000 kilometers of cycling paths cross the region making this a paradise for riders of perfectly signed paths.

6.4. Business Tourism

Upper Austria also provides meeting places for inspiration and motivation.

6.4.1 Convention and trade fair centers

> ➢ 17 Meeting and convention centers
> ➢ 3 exhibition centers and trade fair grounds

6.4.2 Hotel capacities

> ➢ One - 5*-hotel offering 60 beds
> ➢ 116 - 4*-hotels offering 10.270 beds
> ➢ 270 - 3*-hotels offering 14.900 beds

Upper Austria counts a total of 387 hotels with 25.230 beds.

Table 1: Number of overnights for official and business trips in 2006

Number of overnight accommodations for official and business trips in 2006 according to the destination						
Destination	accommodation for short business trips		Accommodation for long business trips		Total	
	1000	%	1000	%	1000	%
Burgenland	63,5	1.1	284,7	3,5	348,2	2,5
Carinthia	183,3	3.1	142,7	1,8	326	2,3
Lower Austria	320,2	5.3	333,1	4,1	653,3	4,6
Upper Austria	438,2	7.3	425,3	5,2	863,5	6,1
Salzburg	433,5	7.2	405,4	5	838,9	5,9
Styria	459	7.6	356,9	4,4	815,9	5,8
Tirol	272,7	4.5	184,4	2,3	457,1	3,2
Vorarlberg	98,7	1.6	270,3	3,3	369	2,6
Vienna	634,3	10.6	336,8	4,2	971,1	6,9
Not classifiable	25,8	0.4	10,8	0,1	36,6	0,3
Altogether	2.929,2	48,8	2.750,4	33,9	5.679,6	40,2

Source: Statistics Austria

7. LINZ

The origin of the name comes from –Lentia-, given by Romanians to their military fortress and is derived from the Celtic –Lentos-, indicating a settlement at the river's bend. Linz is located in the north centre of Austria, is the capital of the province of Upper Austria taking inventory of 190,000 inhabitants. It is qualified of 'hub' of an economically thriving province. (Source: City of Linz)

Figure 6: Linz city map

Source: City of Linz (http://portal.linz.gv.at/ServiceResource/booklet/20080220-1425-2477503330.pdf)

7.1. History

The city has always held a high importance over the past, not only for the East-West path but also for the North-South line which marked the shortest route from the Adriatic to the Baltic Seas. It attests an old existence for historians regained traces from the Neolithic period.

It was alternately the central settlement of the Traun province with a market and customs during the reign of the Carolingians or administrative centre of the province as early as the beginning of the 13th century and centre of the Holy German Roman Empire, under Emperor Frederick III.

Later, the Linz toll counted among the most lucrative sources of income for the Austrian Dukes.

The industrialization started in the second half of the 19th century (shipyard, locomotive factory, textile, and food and luxury food industries) and brought a real turnover for the city, with technological innovations. Steam boats on the Danube (1837/38) were introduced, as well as the construction of the horse-drawn railway, the first railway in Europe, going from Linz to Ceske Budejovice (1832) and Gmunden (1836). Later, the construction of the railroad between Vienna, Linz, Salzburg and Passau created a connection to the Bavarian rail network.

The city was expanded in connection with Adolf Hitler's intention of making Linz an industrial, administrative and cultural centre. The development of the war stalled the majority of the ambitious plans, which mainly came into effect through the construction of the industrial plants, while residential buildings, with the monumental plans for the Danube waterfront and the main boulevard barely realized. As a centre of the armaments industry, Linz experienced air raids in 1944/45 with large-scale destruction. (Source: Schweiger, A., Archiv der Stadt Linz)

7.2. Access

> Air

The Blue Danube Airport is located outside the city and connected to the centre by shuttle services. The Linz Airport offers daily connections to the most important international European destinations such as Amsterdam, Brussels, Düsseldorf, Frankfurt, London, Zurich, Munich, Vienna as well as international airports in Graz and Salzburg.

> Rail

Intercity and Eurocity trains connect to Salzburg and Vienna, and from there to all important European capitals.

> Motorway
  - A1 (Munich-Salzburg-Vienna–Budapest)
  - A8 (Passau-Regensburg)
  - A7 (Prague)
> Waterways

Linz is situated on one of Europe's most important waterways, the Danube, which is linked to the Rhine and the Main. Linz is a popular stopover for cycle tourists on the Danube bicycle path from Passau to Vienna.

➤ Urban transport connections

The city is linked with 9 other communities by the urban transport network.

- Tramways: 3; distance: 21,1 km
- Mountain tramways: 1; distance: 2,9 km
- Busses: 21; distance: 138,0 km
- Electric busses: 4; distance: 19,1 km

TOTAL: 29; distance: 181, 1 km

➤ Parking facilities

In the city center today there are about 6,500 underground garage parking spaces and 6,000 metered short-term parking spaces.

(Source: City of Linz)

7.3. Economy

«   Linz steels the future

Linz develops chemistry

Linz moves technology

Linz thinks innovation   »   (Source: City of Linz)

The first stage of industrialization in and around Linz started through the textile industry. The Linz Metropolitan Area is the hub of a thriving regional economy. Many internationally well-known enterprises have their headquarters in Linz and export high quality products all over the world. The co-operation of the enterprises with university institutions, within the ranges of mechatronic and computing technology, stands for the future orientation of the location Linz. It is the major centre for the production of iron, steel (Voest-Alpine Steel Group) and chemicals. The city administration wishes to support and cooperate with business ventures of all sizes and sectors to erect a flourishing frame and structure to assist the needs of the future businesses. Linz is currently Austria's second largest economic area with over 6,200 businesses and over 191,000 jobs. To face with increasing business expansion, the city of Linz has designed the commercial and business centre South Park Linz (Südpark) in the Pichling district of the city in addition of the existing commercial business centre Franzosenhauspark.

7.3.1. Franzosenhauspark

The park was built in 1989 and currently employs over 1,350 employees and houses businesses ranging from mobile phone providers to furniture stores. (Source: http://www.linz.at/english/business/390.asp9)

7.3.2. South Park Linz

The park represents 330,000 m² of an industrial area zone categorized as an industrial development and combination construction area, located in the south of the city. 140,000 m² zoned and designated for development. The park is easily accessible by streets, water, canals, and full access to water and power lines. In an environmental protection policy, properties are completely free of pollutants, contaminates, and harmful substances and surrounded by greenbelt zones. Currently, 18 well-known businesses are located in the surrounding area: machine construction, trade and business firms, and food retailing industry, software development, and a wood working business. (Source: http://www.linz.at/english/business/394.asp)

Figure 7: City's development map

Source: City of Linz, http://www.linz.at/english/business/394.asp

7.4. SWOT Analysis

Strengths	Weaknesses
<ul><li>Location in the very heart of Central Europe</li><li>Third biggest city of Austria</li><li>Major centre for the production of iron, steel and chemicals.</li><li>Second largest economic area of Austria</li><li>High-tech equipment, venues for up to 3,000 people, hotels for all budgets, gourmet restaurants for all tastes</li><li>Low unemployment rate: more employment than inhabitants</li><li>Population is in majority young</li><li>City on a human scale</li><li>Good public transport connections</li><li>Architecture</li><li>Landscape</li><li>Danube</li><li>Welcoming attitude</li><li>Ecologically oriented</li></ul>	<ul><li>Lack of parking areas</li><li>Lack of hotels especially of large capacity (more than 150 rooms)</li><li>Lack of infrastructure to welcome meetings outside</li><li>Design of Linz centre has image weakness</li><li>Always perceived as second destination</li><li>No direct flight connection to the main European capitals</li><li>Lack of promotion</li></ul>
Threats	Opportunities
<ul><li>Hegemony of Vienna, Salzburg and Innsbruck</li><li>High concurrency from Eastern and Central countries which invest enormously</li></ul>	<ul><li>Be a destination with a change or scene for tourists</li><li>Linz 2009</li></ul>

7.5. Offer

7.5.1. Accommodation

Concerning accommodation, the city offers 50 different possibilities, from luxury 4-star hotels down to youth hostels. The hotel business is ranked as good quality and most hotels are indeed classed with four stars. The city has 13 three-star hotels and 10 four-star hotels. The down town provides 1.679 rooms. Linz hoteliers recorded almost 700,000 overnight stays in 2006, which represents an occupancy rate of over 70%. The industry's aim is to reach the 930,000 mark in 2009. (Source: City of Linz)

7.5.2. Linz City Ticket

The -Linz City Ticket- combines a: restaurant voucher, sightseeing tour on the Linz City Express train, admission to 12 museums, a postcard of Linz, ride with the grotto railway, admission to the Botanical Gardens, admission to the Linz zoo, 20% reduction for a boat trip Linz - Aschach – Linz, 14% reduction (€ 6, - instead of € 7,-) for the daily sightseeing tour of Linz and a railway day ticket to the Hallstatt salt mines. (Source: City of Linz)

7.5.3. Shopping

In comparison with other Austrian cities, with 237,000 visitors every week the main shopping street of Linz, Landstraße, takes second place after the Viennese Mariahilferstraße. Passage Linz, Arkade Taubenmarkt and Atrium City Centre make Linz an attractive shopping city. (Source: City of Linz)

7.6. Culture: Linz, city of the third millennium

"In cultural and education policy, the economic, social and cultural development of the city aims to strengthen an intact cultural and information society". (Source: Dr. E.Watzl, Dr. F. Dobusch, Dr. J.Pühringer; Linz 2009. Application for European Capital of Culture)

Culture has a long tradition, as early as 1569, the first opera was performed to permanently establish the -State Theater- in 1803.

7.6.1. Independent art scene

Culture is a main focus in the city's development. Linz has created an independent art scene to establish, comfort and impulse its know-how in this domain which became key point of the Cultural Development Plan guideline.

The independent art scene comprises alternative cultural initiatives as well as small, independently working artistic teams. This independent art scene also contributed substantially to the success of the European Culture Month 1998. (Source: City of Linz)

7.6.2. Volkshaus

The community centers of Linz, the –Volkshaus- or -house of the people-, are important interfaces for cultural work in the districts of the city.

A total of fourteen of these community centers are the most highly frequented meeting points in the Linz city districts for events and activities of all kinds. Over 300,000 guests visited these community centers in 2006. (Source: City of Linz)

7.6.3. European month of Culture

The European City of Culture project was launched, following Melina Mercouri's initiative, by the Resolution of Ministers responsible for cultural affairs meeting on 13 June 1985, in order to contribute to bringing the people of Europe together. The European Cities of Culture have been chosen until 2004, on an intergovernmental basis meaning that the Culture Ministers meeting at the Council of the European Union selected cities worthy of hosting the event, taking into account parameters. By a resolution adopted in 1990, Culture Ministers meeting at the Council of the European Union set up a new cultural event, namely the -*European month of culture*- taking place each year in a city of a European country based on democracy, pluralism and State law principles. Actually, this event was for the benefit of countries of East Europe at a very specific period of their History.

Linz was elected European month of culture in 1998. Thus, 2,000 artists developed and created more than 30 projects. The event attracted more than 4,000 visitors between the months of August and October 1998. The city was focused on the rapid transformation of work, information technology, science and society. This event pushed the city on an international level due to the involvement of international co-operations in the European

Culture Month organization and allowed to establish and renew artistic networks. The city exhibited and enlightens its transformation and in a certain way proved that nothing was impossible, the city is from now on a modern city of culture. At this occasion, the city invited the EU ministers of culture at the Design Centre Linz the ministers of culture from central and eastern European countries to this meeting. (Source: European Capital of Culture)

7.6.4. Brucknerhaus

The Brucknerhaus Concert Hall is nicknamed the "Linzer Torte" built in steel and glass and opened its door in 1974. It is recognized as a cultural and architectural landmark and has become a globally renowned concert venue. With guest performances by famous orchestras, such as the internationally known Bruckner Orchestra, soloists and conductors in addition to its the program offer for children, it is committed both to preserving tradition and to introducing contemporary music works in all their diversity. Annual highlights of the program are the Linz Klangwolke, the Bruckner Festival and the Ars Electronica Festival.

7.6.5. Ars Electronica

This point is going to present the diverse faces of the Ars Electronica.

7.6.5.1. Ars Electronica Centre: 'Museum of the Future'

The Ars Electronica centre is a museum dedicated to the electronic arts combining the domains of art, technology and society. It investigates wide-ranging new forms of expression and experience by means of intuitive interfaces, data access, and sensory environments. It is a setting of the convergence of the "power of the real and the virtual". (Peter Higgins Land Design Studio, London)

It has six floors filled with creative work from hi-tech laboratories all over the world.

7.6.5.2. Ars Electronica Festival

Since 1979 the Ars Electronica has been a platform for digital art and media culture that is unique in its specific orientation and many years of continuity. The city receives for example a lot of international media attention as a result of its annual Ars Electronica Festival, an international festival for Electronic Art. The topics addressed by the Ars Electronica festival have stepped beyond the narrow boundaries of arts and focus on specific aspects of the civil society with international interest. (Source: http://www.aec.at/de/festival2007/index.asp)

7.6.5.3. Ars Electronica FutureLab

Located in the same building as the Ars Electronica Centre and is defined as a place for researching and trying out new cyber arts technologies. The laboratory is interactive, multimedia and characterized by completely new approaches to conceptualization and design. (Source: http://www.aec.at/en/futurelab/index.asp?nocache=67631)

It has five main tasks:

> Research and development field: the FutureLab cooperates with universities and private sector associated to performing innovative R&D projects of information and communications technology. The Futurelab's specialty is the development of hardware and software for Virtual Reality applications.
> Conceptualizing and designing exhibitions: the Futurelab stimulates visitors to have a go a lively, handsome experience with high-tech.
> Media for architecture: by developing architecture that establishes
> Interactive relationship with its surroundings and become a visible expression of corporate culture.
> Media art : make technology useful for art, establishing it as an artistic material and helps various artists
> Interactive presentations to make the access to information more quickly and clearly on an attractive way.
> (Source: http://www.aec.at/de/futurelab/index.asp?nocache=185439)

7.6.6. Lentos Art Museum

The Lentos Art Museum provides international collection and changing exhibitions and is considered one of the most important museums of modern art in Austria. The Collection of the Lentos Art Museum comprises nearly 1,500 works from the areas of painting, sculpture and object art, roughly 100,000 works on paper and 1,200 examples of artistic photography. (Source: http://www.linz.at/english/tourism/1028.asp)

7.6.7. Environmental preservation

The city focuses ecology and environment protection is one of the priorities of politics. The city has more than 50% of green belts with a total of 50 parks and leisure areas and has been elected:

> - Since 1986 City of Peace
> - Since 1991 member of the Climate Alliance.
> - Since 1992 member of the network -Healthy Cities of Austria-.
> - Since 1996 member of the task force Danube Cities Economic Region (Source: City of Linz)

7.6.7.1. SolarCity

SolarCity is an urban development project, for which the idea arose in 1990. It has been subsidized by the EU and the province of Upper Austria and designed by internationally acknowledged architects. The project is based on three major pillars of sustainability, namely, economic growth, ecological balance and social progress. The success of the project will not have been effective without a determination of objectives and specification of plans, as well as the institution of a central project management team. The City of Linz adopted a decision to implement low energy construction methods in the field of public housing. At the same time, the population has been awarded that the construction and operation of buildings involving a high consumption of fossil energy was a major contributor to the greenhouse effect. Both factors were decisive arguments in favor of a sustainable ecological urban district concept. The district of Pichling, was the only possible area available for a potential expansion and is characterized by existing estates of single-family houses, smaller bathing lakes and, in the immediate proximity, the Traun-Danube riverside meadows, the largest continuous natural biotope structure in central Upper Austria. (Source: http://www.linz.at/english/life/3199.asp)

7.6.8. Casino

Casinos Austria opened its tenth casino in Linz on 12 March 1982. As a result of its exquisite gastronomical offers and a series of attractive events, for locals as well as for international guests the provincial capital is unthinkable without Casino Linz. The event segment was further expanded in 1997 with the opening in 1997 of a 200 m² event halls, the Casineum. For the occasion of its 25-year anniversary Casino Linz underwent a major refurbishment. Since then Casino Linz has shown resplendent in its exclusive, modern ambience. (Source: http://www.casinos.at/content.aspx?muid=26dae352-0f86-4eed-aca7-cadc3d2c0fff)

8. BUSINESS TOURISM IN LINZ

The economic area Linz has become an attractive location for conferences and congresses. The city owns one of the most famous exhibition and congress facilities in Austria and has the right venues for congresses, meetings, fairs etc.

The city homes:

> 10 event houses
> 11 conference hotels
> 14 houses with seminar spaces
> 18 Event locations
> 8 Danube ships

8.1. Convention & Trade Fair Centers

> Design Center Linz: 20 rooms for up to 3.000 people
> Palais Kaufmännischer Verein: 7 rooms for up to 900 people
> Ars Electronica Center: 4 rooms for up to 120 people
> Lentos Kunstmuseum: 3 rooms for up to 550 people
> Intersport Arena Linz: 4 rooms for up to 7.200 people
> Brucknerhaus: 5 rooms for up to 3.100 people

In 2006, the Design Centre hosted 97 events on 275 booking days with a total number of 190,195 visitors.

In the baroque ambaince of the palace the commercial association enjoyed approx. 85,000 visitors for 124 meetings.

The Intersport arena Linz counted approximately 179,000 guests with 40 meetings. Since June 2006, there is a new meeting center in Linz the Leather Factory. In the opening year attracted already 37 meetings with approx. found. 5,000.

The Lentos art museum was pleased about 18.000 guests, who experienced the special atmosphere with approximately 100 meetings directly at the Danube. The Upper Austrian national museums attracted 42 meetings with approx. 4,100 participants register.

8.2. Structures in charge of the business tourism

The section is going to enumerate and give a short explanations of all organizations implicated in the business tourism.

8.2.1. The convention bureau - Tourist Board

The MICE department of the Linz City Tourist Board independently and free of charge supports: search for locations and hotels, site inspections, individual compiled evening and supporting programs. The Convention Bureau works together with 25 top partner enterprises.

8.2.2. The Design Centre Linz

"The best event location is useless if the structures of the economic area and the city do not match it." (T. Ziegler, Design Centre Linz, see VI)

The city owns a modern and timeless glass palace, an aerial event location with a glass roof made of 3,456 glass panels appointing the congress centre. The building provides flexible room solutions that offer the same ideal conditions for fairs, congresses, incentives, galas or events with all the standards required for event technologies. The location management policy is to underline the "One face to the customer". All-in-one offers, including other locations and all important elements for an event. Most important goals of business tourism are professionalism, competence and quality. The Design Center sets standards for event technologies and offers for example HD presentation, 16:9 projection, 3D projection, laser shows, digital light and sound technologies, as well as modern screen management. The Design Center Linz BetriebsgmbH was founded in 1990 and is owned by 13 shareholders:

Stadt Linz	48,5%
RHG Holding N.V.	12,5%
Linzer VeranstaltungsgmbH	5%
Reed Messe Salzburg GmbH	5%
Linzer Ausstellungsverein	5%
Agrolinz Melamin GmbH	5%
PCD Polymere GmbH	4%
Voest Alpine Stahl GmbH	3,5%
Raiffeisen Beteiligungs- & HandelsgmbH	2,5%
Bank für Arbeit und Wirtschaft AG	2,5%
Spitz KG	2,5%
Voest Alpine Industrieanlagenbau GmbH	2%
Voest Alpine MCE GmbH	2%

Source: Design Center

The Design Center building was constructed by the city of Linz and its operation was assigned to the Design Center Linz BetriebsgesmbH on the basis of an annual lease.

The Design Center has:

➤ 2,650 seats

➤ 450 cornered tables

➤ 110 high tables

➤ 120 round tables

➤ 36 coat stands for 2,000 people

➤ 50 desks

➤ Catering

➤ Kitchen (3,000 meals per hour, 10 chefs)

➤ Cafeteria

➤ Fair buffet

➤ Restaurant

➤ 440 underground car park spaces, 215 open-air

➤ Car rental companies nearby

➤ 6 automatic ticket machines

➤ 15 automatic barriers

Table 2: Design center's room capacity

	Rooms	sqm	length in meters	width in meters	height in meters
Ground floor	Exhibition Hall	4.300	97,0	47,0	6,5 - 8,5
	Event Hall	1.170	28,8	43,0	6,5 - 8,5
	Convention Hall	650	36,5	17,5	3,2 / 7,2
	Foyer West	550	60,0	14,0	6,5 - 8,5
	Foyer East	550	60,0	14,0	6,5 - 8,5
	Middle Foyer	240	12,6	18,0	3,2
	Rental Office 1 and 2	je 65	10,6	6,0	2,6
1st Floor	Gallery	1.300	58,0	24,0	3,8
Basement	Seminar Room Complex	je 230	20,7	10,9	3,5
	Split Meeting Room 1-10	je 32	7,1	4,5	2,6
	Split Meeting Room 11	82	9,3	8,7	2,6

Source:
Design Center

8.2.2. Bergschlößl

The Bergschlößl at Froschberg, built in 1718, is a renovated baroque castle combining modern comfort and history. It is a location for special requirements. The capacity is for 2 to 250 guests. The castle is located in a 30.000 m² park, founded for the purpose of a botanical course, of the Northern Collegiate (today Aloisianum), first economic-botanical gardens of Upper Austria.

Table 3: Room dimensions and capacities of the Bergschlößl

	Rooms	sqm	length in meters	width in meters	Height in meters
2nd floor	Froschberg	145	17,80	8,20	5,10 (cupola)
1st floor	Pöstlingberg	71	11,20	5,90	3,10
	Oktagon	55	6,90	10,00	3,20
	Gründberg	35	5,90	6,00	3,30
	Kalvariberg	29	5,90	4,90	3,30
Ground floor	Römerberg	61	11,00	5,60	2,80
	Sala Terena	48	9,40	6,20	3,00 (arch)
	Pfenningberg	33	5,60	5,80	3,00
	Bauemberg	35	5,60	6,30	3,00
Remise	Glasfoyer	121	27,70	3,18	3,30
	Kilikion	76	10,40	7,10	2,90 (arch)
	Küche	34	4,50	7,30	2,90

Source: Design Center

Table 4: Activities of the Design Center and Bergschlößl

	2006	2007
Meetings	226	Design Center: 88 Bergschlößl: 133
Congresses	170	
Events	48	
Visitors	200.215	Design Center: 210.644 Bergschlößl: 6.619

Source: Design Linz Center, Mrs. Angelika Gasteiner

Design center Linz BetriebsgesmbH (including the Design Center and the Bergschlößl)

Table 5: Activities of the Design Center and Bergschlößl

In Euros	2007	2006
Sales revenues	**3.593.765,31**	**3.742.529,71**
Charges	3.587.621,38	3.692.850,64
Company earnings	6.143,93	4.9679,07

Source: Design Center, Mrs. Gasteiner

9. KEY FACTORS OF SUCCESS

9.1 Lille

Like many secondary tourist destinations in France, Lille joined forces with the capital, Paris, Maison de la France and with the club named -Tourism in Life-. Those allow these destinations to lead actions on secondary and widespread markets as well as to collaborate and exchange know-how and tools in leisure as well as business tourism. Lille is associated to the organization of conferences between 50 and 1.000 participants and is positioned as a human scale business tourism city. The current trend is to organize smaller meetings, on a more regular basis and more specialized, making the city of Lille an ideal place for these types of meetings.

Lille's goal was to change its image by

> ➢ Creating a slogan
> ➢ Creating a guide
> ➢ Creating a corporate identity to strength the image and position a city
> ➢ Communicating a strategy to make the difference and be unique and based on 5 pillars : access, business capital, friendliness and happiness, cultural and historic city, youth and dynamism.
> ➢ Creating a logo Lille Metropole Europe used on internet, publicity, publications, trades and fairs and customer-oriented marketing
> ➢ Using newsletter to reach the targets such as congress organizer, associations... and inform them about the destination Lille.
> ➢ Using internet
> ➢ Editing MICE pictures
> ➢ Promoting the city to increase the fidelity, develop the reputation
> ➢ Working together with all partners such as transport and logistic societies
> ➢ Introducing a data base management
> ➢ Participating in well-targeted fairs and meetings such as EIBTM, Bedouk, IMEX and alike.
> ➢ Creating an association network (ICCA, ESAE, EFCT, UIA, MPI) and international network thanks to Maison de la France

> ➤ Analyzing and distinguishing market and potential customers, working together with Lille Metropole Development Agency

9.1.1. Pertinent approach and communication strategy

Lille revealed a clever and pertinent approach and its communication strategy was organized by local and territorial actors around a major event: the opening of the TGV line Paris/London to prospect and attract new customers. The British, Belgian and Dutch markets were targeted.

Another relevant element is the fact that the candidature of the city was accepted to become European capital of culture in 2004, which considerably increased the number of tourists and, of course the fame, thanks to an important mediation. Lille could little by little draw attention to a city hardly or not at all and thought to be industrial, dark, cold and boring-and simply changed its image giving itself and gave a new perspective and face.

In terms of congress activity, new equipments have been created and well adapted to the market being aware of the market reality, in term of hotel capacities and other features. Nevertheless, since, hotel capacity has been improved.

Obviously, the engagement taken to develop the city and changes occurred without being able to predict what could happened, lead to some difficulties such as for example, the offer clearness and readability, partially solved by project put into perspective.

9.1.2. Team-work and human mobilization

> "When a congress is organized in Lille, the city makes all services available to satisfy the participants." (Mrs Vitel, Chamber of Commerce and Industry, see p.VI)

The success of Lille could not occur without a team work. Indeed the tourist office, regional tourist and departmental tourist boards elaborated a program as part of an objective convention, signed with partners. Thus, allowed to have better competitiveness, they attend not only professional fairs all around Europe but also canvass operations or promotional actions and present the city's offer. Furthermore the private local actors such as hoteliers, restaurateurs, restaurateur club of Lille and the chamber of commerce and industry became aware of the importance of the scope and gave their support to the project. All energies were mobilized to deepen the common knowledge.

Economic, cultural and tourist sectors are in symbiosis. A real reflection is done upstream to imagine how the destination could be improved and react to the market variation and make decisions as a consequence, as an example, so that all local organizers are supported in their actions.

The Lille Convention Bureau was in created in July, 2006 by
- Chamber of Commerce and Industry of the European community
- Lille Grand Palais
- Tourist Office
- Lille

Memberships are being held by: Hoteliers Club, -the Table Gourmande-, professional club, participating and working together with the convention bureau.

9.1.3. Meeting guide

Produced and published by the tourist office and the Hoteliers Club the meeting guide is a useful tool for congress organizers, providing all tourist offers and possibilities embellished with pictures to attract the visitors. The meeting guide 2008 accesses the communication on 5 key elements:

- Accessibility
- Friendliness
- Inventive
- Leading destination
- Culture

The « Meet in Lille 2008 » has been published in 12000 exemplars and will be distributed to:

- All contacts of Lille Convention Bureau
- All bureaux of Maison de la France
- French consulates and embassies outward
- Air France

The following different professional fairs and workshop are participated in salons such as BEDOUK (Paris), EMIF (Brussels), IMEX (Frankfort), EIBTM (Barcelona), CONFEX (London), CONFEC, M&I, APIM: MAPIC, ITB Berlin, etc.

9.1.4. Lille 2004

Lille 2004 is the best example of idea fusion and an efficient tourist marketing and cultural marketing have been performed to bring in the city. The whole conurbation shared in the honor, and this provided an opportunity not only to speed up the building of cultural facilities, but also to distribute them widely amongst the urban areas. This also led to a major change in image and reputation in France and abroad.

9.1.5. Image

Cultural profusion, contemporary, different, moved of which the destination of Lille managed to present in France and in Europe and state its image.

9.1.6. Conviviality

Lille is reputed for its hospitality and generosity. Foreigners are usually very warmly welcomed in Lille.

9.1.7. Accessibility

The TGV connection is one of the most determinative elements, making Lille an interesting destination. Indeed, the project aims to lead one of the most innovative transports to Lille have not been easy. Pierre Mauroy, mayor of Lille at this time and ex Member of Parliament was the key person who influenced the decision to make a stop in Lille for the TGV connection between Paris and London. Since 1992, Lille has become an important crossroad thanks to the TGV connection, nowadays considers as the first European rail hub with more than 20 returns between Paris and Lille, more than 10 between Roissy-Charles de Gaulle and Lille. Lille is located 45 minutes in TGV from Paris, 80 minutes from London and 38 minutes in Thalys from Brussels.

9.1.8. Congress centre

At the early nineties the actual congress centre has been envisaged to meet several market needs:

> ➢ need of a zenith
> ➢ need of a new space for meetings bigger, more functional, more easily accessible from the motorway and station
> ➢ need of an exhibition area (Lille Grand Palais has been built on the old fair area of 5.000 m²)

The idea was to build one complex with all these commodities instead of spreading the welcoming structures and complicate their access. Nowadays, the exhibition area of 18.000 m² is too small for an agglomeration of 1,300.000 inhabitants compared to the city of Lyon having 6, 7 times this area, so be it 110.000 m². The congress centre is the symbol and pride of the city and an incontrovertible element of its development.

9.1.9. Taking risks

The real beginning of Lille as an innovative and attractive city has been taken in 1995 when the city has dared to present itself for the Olympic games of 2004. Even if the city wasn't winner of the competition, the candidature of such an event had good impacts on the city's image and Lille has developed a strategic campaign very successful in boosting morale, image and social cohesion .France decided to support its presentation and has beaten Paris and Lyon. For the first time, foreigners looked where this city was located. The city gained not only a national but also an international credibility. It has been a turning point in the history of the city.

9.1.10 Consequences

Lille nowadays is very well serviced and is accessible by: train, motorway, air from all the European main cities. Lille is still in expansion and becomes more and more important. Some towns are associated to Lille, such as Lomme since 2000 or L'île Saint Maurice, absorbed by Lille and is one the 10 districts of the city. A second station has been built named 'Lille Europe' few minutes from the existing station –Flanders-. A business district has been created within 5 to 6 years and is a kind of mini –Défense-, the famous business district in Paris, including administrative offices, chair of companies, savings bank chair, 2 stations, Lille Grand Palais, shopping complex and the construction of the Casino Barrière (to be achieved in 2008). The city intends to develop its business district by constructing Euralille 2 including 22 additional hectares between Lille Grand Palais and the station Saint-Sauveur. This sector will include numerous grassy areas, 600 accommodations, office buildings and 10.000 additional m² for the Grand Palais bridged over a deck in order to implement new buildings. The total area of the Grand Palais will be 28.000 m². The convention bureau was created in July, 2006 and is committed to the business activity.

Figure 8: Lille's district in the future

	Romarin
	Lille centre
	Saint Maurice
	Chaude Rivière
	Euralille 2

Source: SAEM (http://www.saem-euralille.fr)

9.1.11. Improvements

- ➢ Hotel infrastructure
- ➢ Increase the welcoming capacity by building new hotels, thinking about the possible welcoming capacity by anticipating the occupancy rate
- ➢ Congress centre: will it aims to fulfill the demand and divides up the events?
- ➢ Enlarge the international communication about the business tourism offer for professionals to attract international customers by means of mix marketing and business to business strategy.
- ➢ Budget not enough weighty.
- ➢ Improve parking facilities and taxi
- ➢ Ameliorate road signs
- ➢ Increase the number of shuttles
- ➢ Provide exhibitions in English

9.2. Linz

9.2.1. European Culture Month 1998

More than 30 projects were developed and realized by over 2000 artists and drew over 400,000 visitors to unusual venues in Linz with contemporary art and culture work. Linz focused on the rapid transformation of work, information technology, science and society during the European Culture Month. It marked the start of the discussion process about the future orientation of the city's cultural policies, which finally led to the formulation of the Cultural Development Plan (KEP) and its guidelines in 2000. (Source: http://www.linz.at/english/culture/4670.asp)

9.2.2. The Cultural Capital's Neighborhood of the Month

Linz consists of a number of informal neighborhoods. Each one of these neighborhoods contributes to the functions of the city on different levels: some offer more jobs, others are more welcoming as regards accommodation or have a better infrastructure or a broader choice of leisure facilities or more open spaces. All these different qualities complement each other making Linz a functional, life-enhancing and colorful city. For the European Capital of Culture in 2009, all the city's neighborhoods are going to participate in the program and help to shape it. (Source: http://www.linz09.at/en/artikel/programm/1345390.html)

9.2.3. Linz 21

The -Linzer Agenda 21- represents a continuous development process and results report. In September 1995 the local council decided unanimously to promote a lasting development of the city Linz. The natural wealth of Linz is to be retained and developed. Aiming to build special city balance, Linz makes its contribution for responsibility for the world climate. Citizens and the local community are to be taking part in the process of the lasting development and the municipal administration should be aligned to future stability. Due to these lasting principles the urban administration was assigned the production of a concrete action program in 1998. In this action program goals and periods are to be defined together with necessary measures, how these goals can be attained. There is a lasting development on the three columns ecology, economics and social developed. They must be compiled therefore hand on a broad basis. In September 2001 the working group was called -Linzer Agenda 21- in the life, in which under the presidency of a representative of the Linzer municipal authorities participated from the most diverse locations as well as external organizations participated. For a following range of topics working groups were established their tasks consisted in the elaboration of lasting guidance goals and sustainability indicators as well as conversion measures. (Source: http://www.linz.at/umwelt/4198.asp)

9.2.4. Sustainability

This subsection treats the plan of culture development and the Upper Austrian regional planning.

9.2.4.1. Plan of culture development (Kulturentwicklungsplan KEP)

Linz culture and cultural policy make a crucial contribution, if it around the town development, which goes to quality of life or around a modern, future-oriented positioning of the urban habitat. With the culture development plan Linz submitted a politico-cultural concept aligned on a long-term basis in the year 2000 as the first Austrian city. In the KEP guidelines for a systematic new positioning of the city Linz are embodied. A vision for Linz as culture and technology city of European dimension technology and new media, open areas, free scene and culture for all was given. An outstanding basis for the application was created at the same time as Linz was named culture capital 2009. A trial balance in 2004 shows so far successfully converted measures:

> Building project art museum Lentos and knowledge tower
> Cross-linking of Linzer cultural facilities, cross-linking of city and country OÖ
> Establishment of the city culture adviser
> Parity: Fixing the parity of women and men in juries, advisers and Kuratorien "symmetry of the sexes": Annual report for the art and culture promotion
> New positioning Linz Fest, development, planning and organization of the festival - 4020 more than music-
> Innovation pot from € 72.000 to the promotion of the free scene
> Creation of promotion agreements of several years for a majority of the free Linzer cultural facilities and culture associations,
> Advancement of the culture of quarters work, cultural quarter stimulation
> Development of the institute for media on the art university Linz
> Project -Linzer urban history 20th Century-

The city also projected a plan entitled -Culture Development Plan 2020-. (Source: http://www.linz.at/kultur/2299.asp)

9.2.4.2. Development of the city

The local development concept is provided on the basis of the Upper Austrian regional planning law 1994 (OÖ ROG 1994). It is a long-term target for the town planning and serves as default for the production of the surface dedication plan. While the local development concept is appropriate by ten years for one period, the surface dedication is specified for a period of five years, offering a basis for the next 10 years of city development from comprehensive research (Source: http://www.linz.at/entwicklung/konzept/entwickl.htm)

9.2.5. Casino

The casino is one of the biggest tourist operations in the city. As casino guests generally do not come to Linz only for gaming, other service providers also profit from the volume of guests at the casino. (Source: Casinos Austria, http://www.casinos.at/content.aspx?muid=26dae352-0f86-4eed-aca7-cadc3d2c0fff)

9.3. Emerging congress destination in general

The author's personal inquiry found out the following outcomes.

The criteria for the survey were chosen according to those enunciated in the Business Travel and Tourism book written by J. Swarbrooke and S. Horner (2003, p. 62-63) specifying that congress destinations have to provide certain conditions in order to be selected, such as :

- ➢ Suitable venue for the meeting
- ➢ Sufficient accommodation if the venue is non residential
- ➢ Attractions for successful social and/or partner programs
- ➢ Good accessibility to the generating market
- ➢ Efficient transport systems within the destination
- ➢ Offer and acceptable level of safety and security for delegates

The author gathered 68 surveys in total and the subsequent tables represent the most important criteria to:

- ➢ Select a destination from both participant's and organizer's point of view
- ➢ Success a congress

All criteria are ordered under a three categories symbolizing the rank in importance for organizing a congress.

1   very important

2   important

3   less important

Table 6: Criteria to organize a congress

Rank 1 (Base: 68 surveys)	Number of answers	%
accessibility	56	82.3
technical equipment	38	55.9
price offer	36	52.9
public transport	31	45.6
Rank 2 (Base: 68 surveys)	Number of answers	%
catering	39	57.3
ambiance	35	51.5
parking	34	50
technological facilities	30	44.1
employees are multilingual	27	39.7
Rank 3 (Base: 68 surveys)	Number of answers	%
interpreter services	28	41.2

Source: author

The most important touchstones to organize a congress are split up into the accessibility, technical equipments, price offer and public transport facilities within the destination.

9.3.1. Venue and location

Table 7: Criteria of attractive factors to select a destination

Rank 1 (Base: 68 surveys)	Number of answers	%
accessibility	53	77.9
price offer	40	58.8
accommodation	36	52.9
image	29	42.6
amiability	28	41.2
Rank 2 (Base: 68 surveys)	Number of answers	%
political situation	29	42.7
activities choice	28	41.2
public transport	25	36.8
Rank 3 (Base: 68 surveys)	Number of answers	%
shopping	38	55.9
cultural aspect	37	25.2

Source: author

On a general scale, J. Swarbrooke and S. Horner (p.135) also mentioned that the image was an important benchmark in marketing business travel and tourism and stated that:

> ➢ Conference and exhibitions organizers and incentive travel agencies choose destinations for their events, partly based on their perceptions of these destinations
> ➢ Conference delegates often choose to attend conferences partly based on the perceived attractions to otherwise of the place
> ➢ Partners choose to accompany business travelers visiting a destination only if they perceive it to be an attractive place

The attractive force of a destination is a blend of several standards as for instance, the countryside, the behavior of locals, safety and security and the infrastructure and price levels.

The survey as well as the expert interviews confirmed this assertion.

" Aujourd'hui quand on choisit une ville de congrès, on ne la choisit pas parce qu'elle a un Palais des Congrès qui est fonctionnel ou parce qu'elle est accessible ou qu'elle se trouve au bord de la mer ou autre, on la choisit pour la destination dans son ensemble ". (Sylvain Caucheteux, Lille Grand Palais)

Table 8: Keys factors of success

Rank 1 (Base: 68 surveys)	Number of answers	%
program	43	63.2
logistic	39	57.3
location, venue	38	55.9
Rank 2 (Base: 68 surveys)	Number of answers	%
catering	34	50
marketing & sales	32	47

Source: author

The three previous tables confirm therefore the affirmation of J. Swarbrooke and S. Horner and enlighten the most important criteria, namely accessibility, accommodation, price, program. Besides, the author found out other important points to be a successful congress destination.

9.3.2. Credibility

Doctors or professors play the role of facilitator during all the duration of the congress. The attendance of such a scientific in the case of a medical congress is important and brings credibility. He is going to lobby, direct and overlook the congress.

9.3.3. Quality

9.3.3.1. Service levels

The service quality plays an important role in the success congress. Indeed, the participant is waiting to be supported during the whole duration of the congress. Accurate information as well as resourcefulness and reliability are key elements.

9.3.3.2. Staff

The quality is defined with a supportive convention bureau in the destination with employees having flexibility language skills and organization. Other points mentioned are the availability, diplomacy, tact, patience, friendliness and professionalism of the employees before, during and after the congress with one interlocutor supervising the entire organization as well as the effectiveness and reactivity of the team to the last minute changes or client requirements. The supports of local authorities to promote and engineer the congress are important. A confidence between clients and organizers has to be established.

9.3.3.3. Catering

The catering is also a key element and the quality of the food and beverage are a vital ingredient. The satisfaction of the participant also depends on meals provided during the congress.

9.3.3.4. Program

An interaction between the scientific part with well known faculty and the Social event part is relevant. The combination of pertinent speakers, time to interact/network between sessions, interesting topics, and originality will be determining factors of success.

9.3.4. Accessibility

The accessibility is one of the most important elements to take into account. Indeed, both delegates and participants are going to consider if the destination is easy to reach or not. From this perspective, not only the straightforward accesses by air or plane from European capitals are significant. Even a destination served by an efficient transport infrastructure is more important than its actual geographical location. Convenience and speed are essential qualities sought by those travelling by air, as delegates are no longer prepared to tolerate long, time-consuming connections at airport to get the destination (R. Davidson and B. Cope; Business Travel: Conferences, Incentive Travel, Exhibitions, Corporate Hospitality; 2003, p.110).

9.3.5. Marketing and sales

The way how to promote and push a destination is considerable. The destination has to find a new idea, something else which does not exist in another place or think about how a novelty could be applied. The destination has to dare and not waiting for the business. For any special and unusual performance, the press will be captivated. One more criterion mentioned is the possible targets for a congress: increasing number of delegates, scientific of other topics and speakers of interest.

9.3.6. Packages

Figure 9: Congress sold as a package

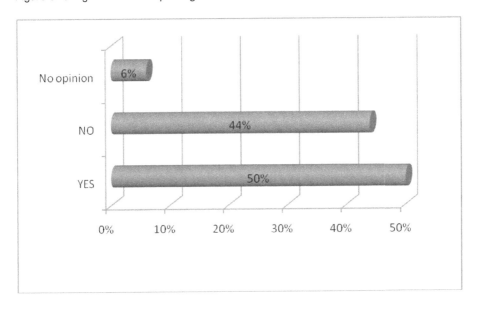

Source: author

The survey revealed that regarding the congress as a tourist product, professionals disagree with much disparity. However, 50% of them agreed on the fact that a congress can be sold as a package.

Basically, in all surveys, the congress package has to include:

➢ Accommodation
➢ Registration
➢ Program
➢ Transfers
➢ Catering (lunches, coffee breaks, dinners, water in the meeting rooms...)
➢ Evening activities, gala event
➢ Eventual sightseeing or other activities
➢ Congress location and facilities

As an example, the congress center of Deauville provides a package including the convention hall with all equipment required, coffee break, lunch break, parking for free as well as in addition the possibility to be accommodated in a three-star or four-star hotel.

9.3.7. Congress center

The author´s survey brought to light that the best place for organizing a congress was when a destination has a benefit of a congress center. 82% of the professionals having participated to the survey agreed and corroborated the assumption.

Figure 10: Perfect place to gather

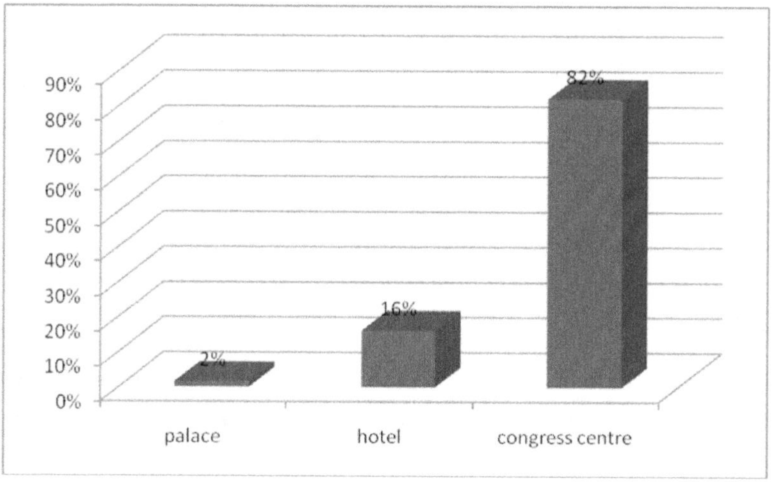

Source: author

10. FUTURE TRENDS

10.1. Internationally

The MPI Future Watch 2008 report has the following expectations for the future:

➤ Meeting planners and suppliers prognosticate a stable market growth for meetings and events with few or no change in overall volume.

➤ Planners predict between 2007 and 2008 an increase in average meeting attendance of 11% for corporate meetings, 18.3% for association events and 19% for conferences.

➤ An augmentation of the number of professional meeting of 19% overall and of 31% in Europe.

➤ Meeting planners foresee an 11% increase in their budgets, corporate planners a 27% increase while association planners a 9.3% decrease.

➤ Use of onsite technologies and web casts more often.

➤ More involvement of the respondents in the shifting goals and strategies within the organizations.

➤ Meeting business increase of 13% in volume is expected.

➤ Responsibility for meetings functions is centralized and the consolidation of meetings and events budgets across entire organization is still arising.

➤ Planners choose to meet more likely city hotels than other venues.

➤ Conference centre and university are chosen by governmental events, more popular in Europe, whereas, convention centers are most likely chosen by association and independent planners.

➤ Meeting professionals envisage a rise in hotel rates of 8%.

➤ Respondents envision the budget, workloads and strategic purpose of meetings as internal trends and economical issues, fuel costs and changing technologies as external trends.

➤ The report also revealed that the most important issues to teach meeting and event industry are to understand better the profession with: procurement and finance

➤ Marketing and communications

➤ Assessment and report of the impact of meetings

10.2. Lille

The Grand Lille committee plays an important role in the city's development. Indeed it analyses all actions and trends in Europe and the world and think about how these could be applied to the city to enlarge the economical and cultural development. The committee displays today of 600 members. Every two months, files are studied and a decision to invest or take certain directions is made.

10.2.1. Lille 3000

In the continuity of Lille 2004, Lille 3000 carries on the dynamism drew, encompassing the world and questions of future, by making full use of the know-how and attributes of Lille Metropole and surroundings. It explores various domains and thinks about the way to link civilization and society by mixing different themes such as: economy and technologies, the conception of the city of tomorrow and of a new lifestyle. Lille 3000 organizes diverse cultural events to perpetuate the diversity of the cultural offer. (Source: Lille 3000)

10.2.2. In a near future

The current trend is always the short-stay market and the decision is taken at the last minute. The professionals have to adapt to this trend and react fast to this demand with, Lille, being a traditional short-stay destination.

10.2.2.1. Federate professionals

The most important objective to be fulfilled over next years is to continue to federate professionals and fusion ideas. Later, the convention bureau would like to create tools such as guides improving their internet website to make the offer more efficient. Finally, they will put in place the prospective and analyze with competent tools the market to fish for congresses.

10.2.2.2. Projects

The current projects presenting as following are going to see the light of day in the next 5 years.

10.2.2.2.1 The Casino Barrière

First, the construction of the Casino Barrière in 2009 with a hotel of 240 rooms and the installation of -Les Galeries Lafayette- give an additional leisure activity for participants of a congress.

The next step envisaged would be the construction of a hotel jumbo jet which could add more opportunities and comfort to the destination, leading the increase of interest and confidence for potential customers. Indeed, the biggest hotel existing in the region is the three-star Mercure hotel located next to Lille/Lesquin airport, counting 250-300 rooms. The fabulous position of Lille between Paris, Brussels and London is not to be neglected and is a real strength to attract European participants. But the hotel offer is not enough to attract corporate or congresses. Lille nowadays has the best occupancy rate in France but the city desperately lacks hotels. When a congress or any events are organized participants are spread off all over Lille instead of being concentrated on the same place.

10.2.2.2.2. Develop a new tour

The Tourism Office intends to develop another thematic tour. The Anglo-Saxon tourists place importance to their ancestors and collect one's thought in silence on graves. The idea would be to create a recollection tour especially for this type of demand and offer as a complement other visits in museums. On the same model as the British Commonwealth, the tour could include not only Lille and the surroundings but also some cities of Belgium such as Ypres. A similar tour already exists since October, 6th 2007 and has so far been a big hit.

10.2.2.2.3. Translation services

The TRANSPOL Company is going to develop machines to buy public transport tickets available in different languages and making the access to the information easier.

10.2.2.2.4. Lille Grand Palais

The fact that a big company installs its chair in Lille is always a victory for the city but it is also known that as soon as the city shall be in recession, these companies could decide to move to another city and that nothing is won. Lille is booming and did not yet reach its maturity phase and professional are aware of this and hope to profit of the situation to attract even more tourists. The congress centre for example intends to reach sales of 18.000 Euros the next two years. But reaching this objective implies increasing efforts and satisfy the clients by offering a higher quality. An extension of the congress centre of 10.000 m² is planned.

10.2.2.2.5. Zenith

The Zenith engaged a program of renovation of its equipments over a period of three years. Changing rooms, spaces of catering and reception hall are going to follow a cure of embellishment. The objectives are set up as following:

➤ To satisfy the public of the Top and to offer to the artists and the producers one always structure more adapted to their needs.

➤ To raise to the challenges of tomorrow.

➤ To amplify its development, the Zenith dashed three challenges. Years to come will see becoming intensified the international opening. In parallel, the links with companies are going to grow rich around the concept Zenith VIP Pass specially conceived for and works councils. Finally, the event sector should know a strong growth.

10.2.2.2.6. Louvre 2

The so-called Louvre-Lens will be located 25 kilometers from Lille and be composed of buildings in glass and aluminum in the heart of a 22 hectares park. The construction and settlement cost is estimated at 127 billions of Euros. The museum should open its door in 2010 and around 500,000 visitors per years are expected. The construction of a Louvre 2 in Lens will be a real springboard for the city of Lille. Lens offer actually is not well developed compare to Lille. Lens has less than 3 hotels at the moment. Shuttles between Lille and Lens could also be implemented. (Source: http://www.nordpasdecalais.fr/louvrelens/intro.asp)

10.2.2.2.7. Olympic games 2012 - London

The city is also taking the Olympic games of 2012 in London as an interesting chance of competitiveness, even if the event is not organized in France. Indeed, the idea is to make a package « accommodation-transport » on a competitive rate, which could be cheaper than a reservation in London. So much as, the idea to organize a universal exhibition in 2012 has been evocated to attract a maximum of tourists in Lille.

10.2.2.2.8. Universal exhibition

From Mrs. Vitals' point of view, Lille was not ready to organize this kind of event and she thinks that the ideal moment to organize it would be in 2017. She also gave advantages that an international exhibition could bring to the destination and what would be the objectives to reach:

> It will not be profitable for Lille but for France too by promoting an image of a France modern and strength it.

> Promote a sustainable construction, the perception of a new architectural and urban style on respect to ecology.

> Re-balance the economical activity and cliché: «the region of the Nord, one of the poorest regions of France » and enlighten its potential by consolidating the esteem of the population.

It also could be an occasion to celebrate and congratulate all efforts undertaken so far to encourage people to continue. The main objective is to revitalize employments on a long-term view and to celebrate the creation of Eurodistrict Lille-Tournai-Courtrai gathering and incorporate into Lille a strategically vision.

10.2.2.2.9. Develop of new markets
> German market

The German market is an interesting and important market on which Lille would like to be positioned. Indeed, Lille is not located far away from Cologne (3 hours) and presents good potential. The possible customers come to see exhibitions and at the moment, just a few Tour-Operators schedule the destination. Professionals actually know that Lille is not located in Normandy and that the city has an airport. The city got some contacts by participating to different fairs and road shows.

> Gay market

The tourist office wishes to develop products adapted to this market and fulfill their needs and waiting.

10.2.2.2.10 Lille-Amiens

Lille Grand Palais won the Amiens invitation to tender and is going to run the future zenith of Amiens at 30 %. The city of Amiens forecasts to build a 6.000 places zenith.

10.2.3. In a distant future

The city intends to develop its tourism on a long-term and sustainable concept.

10.2.3.1. Low-cost

From Mr. Masson's' point of view, the elaboration of low cost connection could be a chance to attract more British customers. Indeed, they are 30% who travel with a low cost company but this does not constitute a priority because of the importance of the TGV. For example, a low cost between Lille-Milan and Lille-Venice have been developed and Italians customers are more and more to visit Lille. To the other side, the line Lille-Warsaw knows more success from French clients than Polish clients regarding the buying power level.

10.2.3.2. Chinese market

The Chinese market is the real next challenge of the city. Charles de Gaulle, born in Lille, hero of the Second World War and president of France from 1958 to 1969, was the first to recognize China as communist. Based on these arguments, Lille could attract Chinese clients. Besides, the historical context, pedagogy and documentation would be used to interest Chinese potential customers.

10.2.3.3. A transborder cooperation

A transborder cooperation with Belgium is also mentioned which would be done on an evident way the next years and could concern common reflections and actions in the tourism field. The idea is to create bridges between the two countries. The tourist board, for example, would like to enable the cities of Courtrai and Tournai of the Tourist Promotion Funds. Moreover the city of Courtrai with Courtrai Expo is one of the most important concurrent of Lille in term business tourism. An alliance could be in favor of both countries.

10.2.3.4. Tourism Observatory

Lille intends to create a business tourism observatory in order to evaluate spillovers in partnership with the convention bureau and the Urban Development Agency. The aim being to touch, get in people and edict their curiosity to make discovering the variety of the heritage and the culture.

In 2007, three to four important personalities have been invited to make an education tour but the budget allocated this year was not sufficient and will be multiply by 10 in 2008.

10.2.3.5. Sustainable development

Agenda 21 engagement:

- ➢ Promote, disseminate and share the culture of sustainable development with the help of films, exhibitions… and train officers.
- ➢ Involve the metropole in the fight against the global warming by drawing up a climate plan
- ➢ Take LMCU policies on board by writing a consultation charter, increasing partnership with associations
- ➢ Design and develop a sustainable city by making environmental quality more widespread, creating a pilot eco neighborhood, extending the use of sustainable techniques   such as rain waters drainage, material recycling… as well as by encouraging and enhancing cycling
- ➢ Integrate sustainable development criteria in an operating framework for procurement commissions
- ➢ Organize a campaign
- ➢ Carry out three projects for developing eco businesses: environmental quality and housing refuse sorting and recycling and organic farming.

Figure 11: 4 levels of action, 3 priority working areas

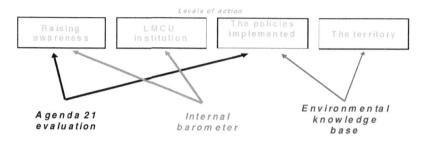

Source: Eurocities, slide 18
(http://www.eurocities.org/liveablecities/site/IMG/ppt/planning_imple
menting___evaluating_LA21_in_Lille__Nov_06_.ppt)

10.2.3.6. Statute change of the tourist office

The tourist office is thinking about changing the statute for a cooperative company to Private Limited Company, allowing it to commercialize.

10.3. Linz

Linz is a world-open city, in which cultural tradition and modern trend live with one another and inspire themselves mutually.

> "Hier geht das momentan Know-how Transfer von Linz nach Wien und nicht umgekehrt. Das heißt, hier wird generiert, hier wird geforscht und hier wird entwickelt. Hier sponsern internationalen Firmen in die Computerwelt." (Eva Wieder, see p.VI)

10.3.1. Linz, European capital of culture 2009, a renewal

> "...And for the year 2009, too, the objectives and ambitions of Linz are clear – as a metropolis of modern media culture and digital arts, as a powerhouse in global networking and communication, as a city embracing new technologies and visions of transboundary artistic activities in an alliance and in partnership with the European Community." (Source: Dr. E.Watzl, Dr. F. Dobusch, Dr. J.Pühringer, Linz 2009, Application for European Capital of Culture.)

As -laboratory of the future- Linz applies as an urban development project as -European Capital of Culture 2009-.

The city aims to maintain:

> A full-time employment and a symbiosis of residential, recreational and employment areas and ensuring local businesses.
> Improve the working environment by providing green spaces and designing attractive and appealing buildings and landscape as well as by combining the work at the office and at home "Telecommuting"
> Secure and expand tourist programs and constructive developments in tourism

Another objective to implement is to reinforce several three-way relationships to promote mutually and stimulating the rich and varied cultural activities:

> Three circles: first Linz itself, second the central area with the cities of Traun, Leonding, Wels Steyr and Enns as larger sub-centers and third the wide circle of the Land of Upper Austria.
> Three regions with their own cultural identity overlap and merge in a both fascinating and exciting process: Mühlviertel, the Bavarian Forest and Southern Bohemia.
> Three countries from the Upper Austrian capital as an intellectual and sensual stimulus: Austria, Germany and the Czech Republic. For Linz and Upper Austria, this will mean significant opportunities for tourism and therefore for the economy as a whole as well as to provide appropriate advance marketing to inform and raise interest and meet the expectations to the promises of high cultural and artistic quality

The city is now creating an appropriate architectural setting for this starring role by expanding the Ars Electronica Centre. The expanded Ars Electronica Centre will feature approximately 6,500 m2 of space, almost 4,000 m2 more than the current facility. There will be more than 120 hotspot areas throughout Linz. This project, realized in cooperation of Linz, LIWEST and Ars Electronica is unique in Austria. A process of sustainability is implemented to establish permanent assets with sustained positive effects for Linz and Upper Austria. The city and the entire region are committed to assuring cultural and artistic quality. Equal acceptance of the artistic visions both sexes, promotion of cultural diversity and the artistic expression of migrant citizens, a commitment to strengthen a humane and culture orientated workplace and support of culture for children and young people promoted earnestly and intelligently.

10.3.2. Constructions

The city already begun to renovate some buildings but in order to accompany its renewal the city builds new infrastructures.

10.3.2.1. Musiktheater am Volksgarten

The regional theatre has a functioning ensemble theatre and repertory theatre for Upper Austria. From its artistic structure and competence the regional theatre could position itself as the most interesting and most innovation-joyful Austrian theatre beyond Vienna. The decision was a matter to meet the self-conception of Upper Austria and positions the province as a modern, future-oriented, art and culture. The theater stands for all forms of the opera (Classic and big opera), works of 20 centuries, contemporary opera, operetta, musical (own-label records as well as appearances), ballet evenings and dances, children's opera and children's musical as well as lieder recitals and choral concerts.

10.3.2.2. Ars Electronica Futurepark

The project of the Ars Electronica Futurepark aims to create a striking landmark amidst the Linz cityscape through the way it blends the new structure with the existing one. As for the building's users, this project's outstanding solution by providing an efficient physical setting for the organization's day-to-day affairs as well as an attractive venue for exhibitions and public gatherings garnered high praise. The dominant theme of the planning concept is the addition of a piece of architectural sculpture to the existing structure. The uniqueness is that it can be directly experienced as a walk-through work of art.

10.3.2.3. Science Park at Johannes Kepler University Linz

"With up to 800 most modern high tech workplaces in the full development the Science becomes a park Johannes Kepler University, therefore into the dynamic centre for research and development in Upper Austria. " (Source: Rudolf Ardelt, rector Johannes Kepler Universität Linz)[1].

Together with Johannes Kepler University and the authorities of the city of Linz a coordinated master plan for a town planning contest was written out in April, 2005 which Caramel architects from Vienna won. It enclosed the town planning solution for the whole project as well as an architectural redraft for the first section. The project is designed in five steps. Nearly 100 million Euros are budgeted for the whole project. For the middle of 2009 the removal of the department of Mechatronik with about 250 workplaces is planned in the moderns fitted out first building. With the design of the first construction step the bases for the realization of the other construction steps were also already created. Special urgency possesses construction step II in the course of from the economy and the technology country of Upper Austria support of development of the technical scientific faculty Johannes Kepler University. The building will home the institute of mathematics, of electronics of information as well as the Johann Radon Institute for applied mathematics of the Austrian academy of the sciences. In the final development it should unite a park of approx. 48.000 m² of so far evacuated institutes or departments, research equipments as for example competence centers, spin off firms from the enterprise establishment program of the JKU and enterprises from the area of Research and development.

10.3.3.   Airports   Council   International   -   March,   2009
ACI has 580 members operating over 1647 airports in 175 countries and territories. In 2006, ACI members handled 4.4 billion passengers, 85.6 million metric tones of freight, and 72.2 million aircraft movements. The international congress will be organized in Linz and will mark in the future market, future perspectives for the city.

---

[1] "Mit bis zu 800 modernsten High-Tech-Arbeitsplätze im Vollausbau wird sich der Science Park der Johannes Kepler Universität somit zu dem dynamischen Zentrum für Forschung und Entwicklung in Oberösterreich entwickeln". Translated from German by the author.

10.3.4. Design Centre

Focus of the future strategy in running the Design Centre as a DMC (Destination Management Company).

"Firmen und Verbände die hier noch wissenschaftlich tätig sind, die hier in ihren Prozessen bei Kongressen wissenschaftlichen Themen ausarbeiten und kommunizieren, die haben in Linz sehr gute Nährboden" ... (Eva Wieder, 2007, see p. VI)

..."Die Stadt als Kongressdestination indem hinsichtlich der Qualität für das internationales Publikum und der Standards abgestimmt ist. Das Design Center hat hohes Niveau und Standard. Das gehört aber auch parallel in einer Linie mit der Hotellerie, der Gastronomie, dem Handel und den Geschäften abgeglichen. Das muss durchgehend sein wie ein roter Faden. Diese Qualität muss auch gelebt werden." (Eva Wieder, 2007, see p. VI)

10.4. Future trends in general

According to the experts:

> Only congresses with an excellent scientific programme and "hands-on workshops" will survive. All other congresses will be carried out via tele conferences, Internet platforms.

> People will want to attend more comprehensive (week-long) congresses with top speakers, but fewer congresses in total during the year. There will be more joint conferences made between different networks/organizations to save on organization costs, speakers, etc.

> Congress tourism will become more important, but due to the restrictions of pharmaceutical companies it will become more and more difficult to add touristic points like sightseeing to the program.

> A very specialized congress has to compete with other options of continued education (online etc) and therefore needs to emphasize on networking and interactivity.

> Unexplored venue as everybody gets tired of the same destination again and again. People have to be brought where they would not be able to go by themselves.

> Sustainability, green meetings as well as virtual congresses and virtual communication are increasing
> More travel, more relations in business as we all have figures of the added value of the congress economy we all are working, marketing & selling our conference & incentive destination.
> The corporate sector and their conference business always goes hand in hand with the economical situation - ROI return of investment becomes more and more important, whereas the association business is relatively secure. We know that there will be a lot of new and investing Asian destinations coming up so for Europe it will be challenging to hold the market shares.

10.5. In summary

> Encourage journalists and potential customers to visit the destination and bring media on regional events.
> Develop quality standards and various offers
> Continue to modernize equipments of the congress centre by investing regularly to maintain a high quality offer and be able to face to the concurrence on the business tourism market by reacting fast
> Be a predecessor of a trend on a market and be in advance compare to the concurrence
> Develop the offer with a sustainable development vision and manage all environmental, consummation rules.
> Consider all the facets of tourism and their implications
> Enlighten the advantages of the destination
> Surprise
> Improve the welcoming service
> Encourage customers to stay longer
> Bounce on opportunities which turned up.
> Remain flexible in reaction to new tourist trends.
> Increased influx of visitors from outside the German-speaking countries.
> Increase in shorter holidays each year, demands for higher quality accommodation and city tourism.
> Warm welcome

> Plan policies
> Improve quality standards and diversify the incoming tourist country of origin.

11. COMPARISON BETWEEN THE TWO CITIES

Similarities	
Lille	**Linz**
Triangle Lille-Roubaix-Tourcoing	Triangle Wels-Steyr-Linz
Euralille	South Park
P.Mauroy, mayor of Lille until 2001and President of the Urban Community of Lille Metropole	F. Dobusch, mayor of Linz since 1988
P.Mauroy and F. Dobusch, development's initiator and key element in the success of their city.	
Grand palais	Design Center
European capital culture 2004	European capital culture 2009
University of Lille	Johannes Kepler Universität
Lille3000	Culture Development Plan 2020
Industrial cities Culture orientation Casino Well-developed transport connections Dynamic Youth city Airport connections Welcoming and friendly atmosphere Shopping facilities Investments in infrastructure	
Differences	
Lille	**Linz**
220.000 inhabitants	190.000 inhabitants
Grand Palais, WTC, CCI, Convention Bureau – related to the congress meeting sector	Design Center-Bergschlößl, tourist office – related to the congress meeting sector
Grand Palais: 22.000 sqm Welcoming capacity until 50.000 persons "One in all" building with exhibition area, zenith, conferences 2007: more than 1 millions visitors 12,7 millions of Euros of sales revenues	**Design Center:** 10.000 sqm Welcoming capacity until 3.000 persons cfdffdd "One face to the customer" offer-flexible room solutions 2007: more than 200.000 visitors 3.5 millions of sales revenues
Lille Grand Palais has a surface area twice as large as the Design Center and is expected to be enlarged by another 55.000 m². The Grand Palais facilities can host 16 times as many visitors and attracts 5 times more people than the Design Center. However, the sales revenues of the Grand Palais are only 3 times more than the Design Center.	

12. CONCLUSION

The investigation is aimed at offering a global image of the factors of success of an emerging congress destination and its future trends. Emerging destinations have to gather some characteristics in order to become potential destinations attractive for congress meetings:

- ➢ Accessibility
- ➢ Adequate infrastructure
- ➢ Approachable and strategic by setting pertinent communication equipments
- ➢ Team work

Linz and Lille display a strangely high number in similarities. At the moment Lille has a higher notoriety than Linz, especially because the city has already been benefitted by the impacts of its nomination as European capital in 2004 and implemented its know-how these past four years.

Both cities are booming and are therefore prosperous potential markets to organize congress meetings, not only because of their cultural offer but also due to the joined work of politicians, tourism professionals and locals who combine their cognizance to develop these cities into touristic destinations. However, the development has to be supported by financial capitals and investments according to the type of market.

Future congress meetings will tend to gather people on a smaller scale and more regularly. Therefore, emerging congress destinations have better opportunities to attract companies that seek to hold small congress meetings in a more convenient place. In addition to this, well-located destinations equipped with suitable convention centers have more possibilities to be a focus for associations and independent planners.

The researcher collected information on the business touristic market in both cities. Nevertheless, the congress industry being relatively young, has made the search of data more complex, and as a result does not allow the collected data on the sector to be yet performed.

REFERENCES

Books

Carey,T. (1999). *Professional Meeting Management: A European Handbook*; Brussels(B).Meeting Professionals International.

Davidson, R. (1994). Business Tourism. London

Davidson, R., Cope, B. (2003). Business Travel: Conferences, Incentive Travel, Exhibitions, Corporate Hospitality and Corporate Travel. 2nd ed. Harlow (UK): Pearson Education.

Denney,R.(1990). *Conventions, Expositions, and Meetings Industry.* New York: Van Nostrand Reinhold.

Denoune, M. (2004). Le média congrès. Réunir pour réussir. Edition de l'Aube, La Tour d'Aigues: Le Moulin du Château.

Dobusch, F., Mayr, J. (1997). *Stadt der Arbeit und Kultur.* Publication :Gutenberg-Werbering. SPÖ Linz-Stadt.

Holloway , J. C. (2002). *The Business of Tourism.* 6th ed.; Harlow: Pearson Education.

Polivka, E.G. (1996). *Professional Meeting Management.* 3rd ed.Birmingham/Alabama. (USA): Professional Convention Management Association.

Porter ,M. (1998). Competitive Strategy: Techniques for Analyzing Industries and Competitors. 2nd ed. Riverside: Free Press.

Rogers,T. (2003). *Conferences and Conventions: A Global Industry.* Oxford (UK):Elsevier Butterworth Heinemann.

Swarbrooke, J., Horner, S. (2002). *Business travel and tourism.* Oxford : Butterworth-Heinemann.

Veal, A.J. (2006): *Research Methods for Leisure and Tourism.* A practical guide, 3rd Edition, Prentice Hall.

Weber,K., Chon,K. (2002). *International Research and Industry Perspectives.* New York, NY [u.a.]: The Harworth Hospitality Press : Longman.

Wöber, K. W. (2002). *City tourism 2002.* Proceedings of European Cities Tourism's International Conference in Vienna. Wien: Springer Verlag.

Websites

About Austria; Austria Travel Guide ; < http://aboutaustria.net/ access >, Access: 24th Jan.2008

ACBN- Austrian Business and Convention Network (2008); < http://www.abcn.at/>, Access: 7th May 2007

Access (2008); Access 2008; <www.access-austria.at/aussteller/default.asp?smid=2&lang=2&exhid=53>, Access: 28th Jan. 2008.

Assemblée des chambres françaises de commerce et d'indiustrie (2008) ; <http://www.acfci.cci.fr/>, Access : 31th Dec.2007

Assemblée nationale (2008); <http://www.assemblee-nationale.fr/12/pdf/rap-info/i2826.pdf >, Access: 31th Dec.2007

BMWA (2008); Bundesministerium für Wirtschaft und Arbeit; <http://www.bmwa.gv.at>, Access 3rd Dec. 2007

Casino Austria (n.p.a); Casino Linz; <http://www.casinos.at/default.aspx?muid=039feaaa-16aa-4143-b04c-d6ece6c62ca>, Access: 24th Feb. 2008

CIC Convention Industry Council (2004); Convention Industry Council; <http://www.conventionindustry.org/ >, Access: 7th May 2007

City of Linz (2008); Linz Welcome; <http://www.linz.at/english/tourism/>, Access: 7th Apr. 2007

EIBTM (2008); the global meetings & incentives exhibition; <http://www.eibtm.com/files/eibtm06micereport.pdf≥, Access 3rd Dec. 2007

Eurocities – the network of major European cities (2008); <_http://www.eurocities.org>, Access: 8th Feb. 2008.

European Capital of Culture (2008); <http://ec.europa.eu/culture/eac/ecocs/present_cap/retrospective_en.html>, Access: 2nd Feb. 2008

Federal Chancellery of Austria (2008); <http://www.austria.gv.at/site/3327/Default.aspx>, Access: 28th Jan. 2008.

France Congrès Association (n.d.a) ; <http://www.francecongres.org/index.htm>, Access : 7th Apr. 2007

ICCA (2005-2007); ICCA - International Congress & Convention Association; <http://www.iccaworld.com/>, Access: 7th May 2007

INSEE-Institut National des Statistiques et des Etudes Economiques (2008); INSEE Nord-Pas-de-Calais ;<http://www.insee.fr/fr/insee_regions/nord-pas-de-calais/rfc/docs/P07_23b.pdf>, Access : 23rd Dec. 2007

Lille Grand Palais (2005) ; Palais des Congerès de Lille ; <http://www.lillegp.com/lillegp/lillegp.htm>, Access : 7th Apr.2007

Lille   Métropole   Tourisme   (1999);   Lille;   <http://www.destination-lille-metropole.eu/FR/arbodyn/affaires.aspx>, Access: 1st May 2007

Lille Métropole Tourisme (n.d.a); <www.destination-lille-metropole.eu>, Access: 8th Feb. 2008.

Lille 3000 (2008); <http://www.lille3000.com>, Access: 15th Aug 2007

Linz   2009   (2008);   Linz   2009   European   capital   of   culture; <http://www.linz09.at/en/detailseite/programm/programm/ankuendigungen09/133146 8.html>, Access: 15th Aug 2007

Mairie de Lille (2008); <http://www.mairie-lille.fr/sections/site-en>, Access: 23rd Dec.

Meeting   &   Conventions   (2008);   m&c   online   meetings   and   conventions; <http://www.mcmag.com/MCMediakit/MCMediaKit.pdf >, Access: 4th Dec. 2007

Ministère   délégué   au   tourisme   (2007) ;   Panorama   du   tourisme d'affaires;<http://www.tourisme.gouv.fr/fr/navd/mediatheque/publication/economie/pa norama_tourism.jsp> September 2002 Edition, Access: 3rd May 2007

Nord pas de Calais (2008); Bienvenue en Nord pas de Calais, Conseil Régional. <http://www.nordpasdecalais.fr/ >, Access: 8 February 2008.

Oberösterreich: Urlaub   in   Oberösterreich   (2008); <http://www.oberoesterreich.at/sommerurlaub.html>, Access: 15th Aug 2007

OJS Office de justification des statistiques (2007) ; <http://www.ojs.asso.fr/site/Accueil-17.html>, Access : 18th Jul. 2007

Promosalons (2008) ; <http://www.promosalons.fr/accueil.php>; Access : 15th Aug 2007

SAEM Euralille (n.d.a); Un outil d'aménagement pour la métropole; < http://www.saem-euralille.fr/>, Access 2nd Feb. 2008

SEM,   Fédération   des   Sem   (2008);   Le   mouvement   d'économie   mixte; <http://www.fnsem.asso.fr/>, Access: 15th Aug 2007

Statistik   Austria   (2008);   <www.statistik.at/web_de/statistiken/tourismus/index.html>, Access: 4th Dec. 2007

Tagungen (2008); Event management, tagung Hotel, Tagungen in Österreich, Oberösterreich;   <http://www.tagung.info/de/warum-oberoesterreich.html>,   Access: 4th Dec. 2007

Tourisme Nord pas de Calais (2008); Comité régional de tourisme Nord-Pas de Calais<http://www.tourisme-nordpasdecalais.fr/upload/hot2006.pdf>, Access: 23rd Dec. 2007

Vienna Convention Bureau (2008); < http://www.vienna.convention.at/> , Access : 7th May 2007

Wien International (2008); <http://www.wieninternational.at/en/node/1041>, Access: 28th Jan. 2008.

WTC (2008); World Trade Center Lille international services and business tourism; <http://www.mairie-lille.fr/sections/site-en>, Access: 3rd Jul. 2007

Magazines and Brochures

ACB-Austrian Convention Business Magazine. Internationales Servicemagazin für Kongress – und Tagungsveranstalter. Austrian Convention Business Magazine. Vienna: Austrian Convention Bureau.

M.I.C.E Lille .(2007). Service Providers and Places in the Nord Pas de Calais Area. D&B Concept Communication. Lille:Le Studio - DB Print

Office du tourisme de Lille, Chambre de Commerce et d'Industrie Lille Métropole, le club hôtelier, le Club des tables gourmandes and Lille Event's. (2005). Meeting Guide Lille Métropole. Office du tourisme de Lille. Lille: Winners

Press releases and articles

Baujard, E. (2007) Euratechnologies : où en est-on ?.Lille on line. Ecole supérieure de journalisme de Lille. 16th March 2007.

Bertrand, L., Lagarde, C. (2006). Mesures pour accroître la compétitivité du secteur foires, salons et congrès. Ministère des Transports, de l'Equipement, du Tourisme et de la Mer; Ministère délégué au Tourisme, 20 Dec. 2006.

Capelle, B. (2006). Lille, à chaque pas une découverte. Lille tourist office

Euralille (1994). Le XXIe siècle en chantier. Lille : Euralille, February 1994.

Grande, K. (2008). Lille Convention Bureau, January 2008

Dr. Laimer, P., Schischeg, C. (2007). Tourism in figures Austria 2006/2007. Statistik Austria. Wien 2007 © STATISTIK AUSTRIA

Lhoest, S. (2005). Lille Grand Palais fête ses 10 ans. Lille Grand Palais, 3 Mar.2005.

MPI (2008). Future Watch 2008: A comparative oultlook on the Business of Meetings and Events.

Vandenberghe, D. (2008). Lille Grand Palais, Un succès maîtrisé. 18 Dec. 2007

Hofmann, M. (2007). Wie Linz bis 2015 zur interessantesten Stadt Österreichs werden will und wie ihr Expo-2002-Macher Martin Heller dabei hilft? In Oberösterreich Nachrichten, 24 Jul. 2007.

Magne, V. tourisme d'affaires: est-on à la hauteur?. In Nord Éclair, 24th October 2007.

Masson, C. (2004). Lille Métropole, une destination de tourisme d'affaires en plein essor. Lille tourist office.

Schmutzhard, H., Mayer-Edoloeyi, A., Sonnberger, E. (2005). Taking stock between KEP 1999 and KH 2009, Discussion of the current situation and future perspectives of the Freie Szene in Linz. Stadtwerkstatt Linz.

Valcke, C. (2007). Création de la CCI Grand Lille. CCI Lille Métropole.

Publications and reports

Charié, J.P. (2006). Le développement en France des foires, salons et congrès. Rapport d'information n. 2826 deposé en application de l'article 145 du règlement par la commission des affaires économiques, de l'environnement et du territoire.

Irion, B. (2000). Les salons internationaux en france: un atout économique indiscutable à mieux valoriser. Commission Spéciale des Congrès et Salons, adopted by the general assembly of 13th April 2000. Congress and fairs Direction of the chamber of commerce and industry of Paris.

Plasait, B. (2007). Le tourisme d'affaires : un atout majeur pour l'économi. Conseil économique et social, République Française.

Mag. Siegbert, J. (2004). Linz 2009. Application for European Capital of Culture. City of Linz, Culture Department

Vilain, C.E. (2007). Strategic Marketing Plan. Lille Métropole Europe Convention Bureau. April 2007.

City of Linz (2007). Jahresbericht 2006. Tourismusverband Linz~Donau.

Commission Développement Culturel. (2002). LILLE 2004 : Facteurs de succès et pièges à éviter. AVIS n° 02.05 CDC – Commission "Développement Culturel". June 2002.

Interviews

Caucheteux, S. (2007). Personal interview about the congress center activity; Responsible for Lille Grand Palais commercial department, November 2007

De Seze, B. (2007). Personal interview about the business tourism in France; project manager- Project and engineering direction at ODIT France, November 2007

Masson,C. (2007). Personal interview about the activity of the congress center; Marketing director of Lille tourist office, November 2007.

Steiner, G. (2007). Personal interview about the tourism in Linz ; Manager of Linz tourist office, August 2007.

Tremmel, I. (2008) : Personal interview about the business tourism in Austria ; Head of abcn, March 2008.

Vilain, C.E. (2007). Personal interview about the business tourism in Lille; Manager of Lille convention bureau, November 2007.

Visintainer, P. (2007). Personal interview about the business tourism in France; Marketing director at Maison de la France Paris, November 2007

Vitel.P. (2007). Personal interview about the business tourism in Lille; Responsable of the tourism - event - congress department chambre of commerce of Lille, November 2007

Wieder, E. (2007). Personal interview about the business tourism in Upper Austria; Themenmanagement "MICE/Kultur/Städte", August 2007.

Ziegler, T. (2007). Personal interview about the business tourism in Linz; Managing Director, August 2007.

CPSIA information can be obtained at www.ICGtesting.com
Printed in the USA
LVOW01s1737230813

349371LV00019B/908/P